Adventures in Analytics

A guide to getting ahead in your Analytics career

C G Lambert

Adventures in Analytics by C. G. Lambert
Copyright © 2023 C.G. Lambert. All rights reserved.
Published by Clamp Limited

First paperback edition November 2023
Typeset in Palatino Linotype

Cover Art by Amir Johnny Nebic
Internal figures by Amir Johnny Nebic
Swirl on front cover by ArtHead-.

ISBN 978-1-914531-50-7 Paperback
ISBN 978-1-914531-51-4 Hardback
ISBN 978-1-914531-52-1 Paperback
ISBN 978-1-914531-53-8 ePUB
www.cglambert.com
www.clamp.pub

Table of Contents

Figures

Preface

Dedication

To all my bosses. The good and the bad.

Introduction

What's In This Book?

Welcome!

This is a book containing career advice for those working in, or wanting to work in, analytics.

I've taken my fifteen-year analytics career and distilled it into a book of ideas, anecdotes and pithy observations that will help shape and guide your own career path.

I've also augmented my experience with the experiences of fifty others, mainly at the senior manager level. Interviewing them has challenged my ideas and given me additional insight into how careers work in analytics.

Who Is This Book For?

This is a book for anyone who has thought: why didn't I get that promotion? Why did that other person in the office get a larger raise? This is for the person who is asked by their parents, "How long have you been doing that for?"

However, this book has insights that are relevant for all technical career paths.

What Won't I Cover?

There's only so much space between these covers, so I won't address career notions that are not specific to analytics. The universal subjects that I will not address include the following:

- How to survive layoffs, redundancy or downsizing
- Managing a bad boss
- Annual Leave not being approved
- Pay disputes
- Working from Home vs Working from the Office
- Sexual Harassment
- How to handle discrimination on the basis of any of the protected classes

It's really important to note that leaving these elements out of the book is not because they are not worth discussing – they really, really are. It's just that I'm not the best person to lead those discussions.

Disclaimer

What follows is one person's opinion and is not legal, financial or investment advice. Use paid professionals who belong to professional industry bodies for advice on legal, financial or investment matters. Your mileage may vary. Success will depend not only on you following the advice within this book, but you must also recognise those scenarios that match your reality and apply the correct actions at the correct time. No warranty is offered. Acting on this advice is at your own risk.

If you feel that your employer may be acting illegally, immorally or unfairly, I cannot help you. Please do not get in touch with me. You need a lawyer who is licensed to operate in your area and has knowledge of the relevant laws. Again, please do not contact me with specific legal questions.

Note on Terminology

I use the following terms interchangeably:

To refer to a **business** as a whole: business, company, firm.

To refer to the part of the business that performs the **analytics** function: org, function, analytics.

To refer to one part of the business: unit, department.

Data is used as a collective singular noun rather than a plural. So, "data is put into a database table," not "data are put into a database table."

IC stands for Individual Contributor. This represents all the roles that do not specifically have a leadership function, and encompasses job titles like Junior Analyst, Analyst, Senior Analyst, Lead Analyst, Principal Analyst.

A **manager** is someone who has management responsibilities. They may also have IC responsibilities, and it's important to identify the IC expectations when applying for a role. The sections in this book which give advice for those who manage people may also apply to those who do not necessarily have manager in their job title. Some ICs also have managerial responsibilities, for example.

Senior managers are the top level of management within the analytics org. They may manage managers, they may interface with other senior management from other parts of the business, or even directly with the c-sphere (CEO, CRO, COO, CDO et al ad infinitum).

Your role title and responsibilities may not match the above. You may be a manager on paper but not have any people management responsibilities. In that instance my advice on IC applies to you. If you are a manager but deal directly with the CEO, you'd probably benefit from reading the sections on senior managers. And if you are the sole analytics employee, you will find that all the advice applies!

Analytics frequently produces dashboards – but not always. When I refer to dashboards I actually mean **artefacts**: those mechanisms for delivering insights to the business. This could be an excel spreadsheet, an email, a web page or a report.

Sometimes jobs reduce the noble art of analytics down to the mechanical provision of one or other of the functions – if all you do is generate data for other people then you might be a **data monkey**. If all you do is create dashboards, then you might be a **dashboard monkey**. It's a derogatory term for the jobs that have been created with a singular focus that removes the variety required to learn the full range of roles within analytics. They are roles in which it is very unlikely you will feel fulfilled, unlikely that you will be recognised for the work that you are doing, and extremely unlikely for you to maximise the business value that you produce.

Political Capital is the ability to get things done and it represents the mana or respect that the business has for a particular person. When you come into a new role you inherit the political capital inherent in the role, but thereafter this increases or diminishes as a result of your interaction with the rest of the business, especially those in senior management. Managing and increasing your political capital is a good way of getting ahead. Sometimes decisions are made solely to maintain political capital (often referred to as, "picking your battles").

I equate the terms **resume**, CV, and curriculum vitae with each other. It's the document you give people to demonstrate the kind of work that you've undertaken, usually in an attempt to obtain a job.

I use some product names as shorthand for their entire category, including their competitors. So, when I refer to **Tableau**, I am referring to any dashboarding product, including direct competitors like PowerBI and QlikView, as well as indirect competition like dashboarding building capabilities in Excel, GSheets or websites featuring d3.js and chart.js.

Likewise, when I refer to **Alteryx**, I also mean other ETL management software regardless of whether it is drag and drop or coded.

P&L means "Profit and Loss," which refers to someone having budgetary responsibilities – usually expenditure, but sometimes revenue as well.

ETL means "Extract, Transform and Load." Because it is so central to data and analytics, a lot of smart people have very strong opinions on how this should happen, which tools should be used and how teams should use these tools. Essentially, it's the process whereby data is moved around the business.

ELT means "Extract, Load and Transform." I believe the point of difference with ETL is supposed to occur where the transformation of the data occurs, however it's also the process whereby data is moved around the business.

Tableau is a dashboarding product that operates as a website with visualisations that can sit either on the cloud or inside a company's datacentre.

A **server** or **service account** is a set of credentials for logging into a program that doesn't identify an individual, but which allows the program to have heightened permissions when accessing other data or performing tasks.

Something is **OnPrem** (or On Prem) if it resides within a firm's datacentre, as opposed to being Cloud-based when it is hosted in the Cloud.

d3.js and **Chart.js** are JavaScript libraries that create charts and dashboards.

A **Propellerhead** (or prophead) is someone who is technically able, but sits in the back office away from anyone else. They are typically someone who is exceptionally smart and socially awkward. I use the term fondly to refer to those who have a technical job but who might miss social cues. It's close to being synonymous with geek or nerd. According to The Web Developer's Journal[1]:

> The term "prophead" is a holdover from the days when the nerd kids on the block wore caps with little propellers on top. This fashion gave way to the pencil pocket protector. Here at the WDJ, "propheads" refers to programmers, developers and other technically oriented types. A weenie doesn't even use a regular keyboard, just a little one with two keys: 1 and 0. Weenies talk among themselves in continuous data streams, which sound to mortal ears like a modem logging on.

---

[1]htttps://www.techtarget.com/whatis/definition/propeller-head-or-propellor-head-prop-head-prophead

I use **UK English**, so those in the US may wonder what all the extra u's are and how those z's have changed into s's. In the UK they use £ instead of $. Pounds instead of dollars.

I use lowercase for **analytics** throughout the book, regardless of whether we are referring to the industry, the function or the department.

I tell you all this so that you don't send me emails telling me that I'm using the wrong word or the incorrect spelling and to ensure that you're prepared for the mental adjustment that might be needed to read this content. I'm sure you'll cope.

Acknowledgments

I was blessed with an abundance of people who generously shared their opinions and anecdotes for inclusion in this book.

Alex Andronic, Min Bhogaita, Mariia Bocheva, Laurence Booth, Jon Chan, Stuart Clarke, Barry Collyer, Nick Creagh, Meercat Dan, Andrew Donald, Max Firth, Antoine Frange, Ioannis Gedeon, Dan Grainger, Jenny Gunn, Adrian Hands, Erin Hartman, Dan Howard, Lukas Innig, Chris Kindon, Corrin Lakeland, Pam Laloi, Rhona MacLennan, Melody Marlage, Rob McLaughlin, Adam Medros, Denver Morton, Peter O'Neill, Dan Portus, Steen Rasmussen, Chris Richardson, Enda Ridge, Gareth Rumsey, Peter Shawyer, Elizabeth Smalls, Simon Spyer, Brian Stuart, Chris S, Sundar Swaminathan, Ada Teistung, Andy Thornton, Francesco Vivarelli, Nico Weyers, Alex Wilkins, Matthew Worsfold, and Caroline Zimmerman.

I was ably aided by volunteers who beta read chapters of the book and whose feedback, challenge and insights were instrumental in making arguments more robust and prose clearer. Thanks go out to Andrew Le Breuilly, David Clutterbuck, Jachen Duschletta,

Elizabeth Hughes, Chris Monger, Denver Morton, Arthur Pritt, Tony Randell, James Ryder, Scott Sealey, Cath & Tom Wolfenden, Alia van Wyk, and Zannat Khandoker.

Peter Shawyer @ Full Circle Recruitment was generous with his time, energy and rolodex, and the insights gained from those to whom he introduced me moved the needle significantly with regards to the senior manager sections of the book.

Peter O'Neill was very helpful in introducing me to people who opened my eyes to the challenges faced in the Agency world, and particularly in the European experience.

I'd like to give thanks to my editor Sally Kilby for her professionalism and consideration.

The interior figures and cover art were done by Amir Johnny Nebic (99designs.co.uk/profiles/johnny572) who has the patience of a saint!

Whilst a large number of people helped me to create this book, all errors and omissions are mine and mine alone.

Finally – as always, thanks to my first reader, Ange.

PART 1

Definitions

CHAPTER 1

What Is Analytics?

Typos are repeatedly highlighted on this manuscript because MS Word thinks the chapter should be titled, "What *are* analytics?" That's understandable, because it thinks I'm asking, "What are the artefacts generated by the analytics department?" "What are the results of the analyses that they conduct?" and, "What are the kinds of things people in the analytics department or function are looking at?" Analytics in those instances is plural because the results of the activities are numerous.

But what I'm interested in is, "What is the *practise* of analytics?" If I am giving advice on careers in analytics, what is this category of work that is called analytics? It's singular because I'm interested in the work function or the type of work that is analytics.

Let's boil all flavours and types of analytical work down to its core commonality. The process consists of the following steps:

Something happens. The event is measured. It is recorded. Then an analyst comes along and does some sort of calculation. The analyst communicates the results.

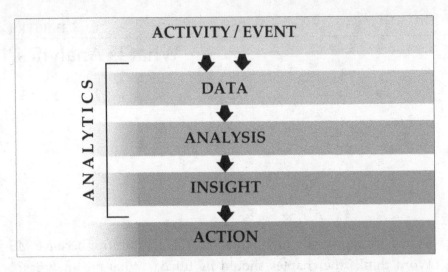

Figure 1 Event->Action

And that's pretty much it. You can change the event that is measured. You can change how it's measured. You can have a huge number of calculations and motivations for the analysis, but it's all analytics.

And analytics as an industry?

If you expand the steps in Figure 1, you can see in more detail what Monica Rogati called the "Data Science Hierarchy of Needs" back in 2017[2].

---

[2]https://medium.com/hackernoon/the-ai-hierarchy-of-needs-18f111fcc007

Who Does It?	What Is It?	Business Value
Data Scientist	Prescriptive Optimisation: What's the best thing to happen?	++++
Data Scientist	Predictive Modelling: What will happen?	+++
Data Analyst	Diagnostic Analytics: Why did it happen?	++
Business Intelligence	Descriptive Analytics: What happened??	+
Data Scientist	Data Cleaning & Structured Data Storage	-
IT	Data Collection & Raw Data Storage	- -

Figure 2 Hierarchy of Needs

The concept that is hardest for some people to understand is that the amount of business value generated by a layer is inversely proportional to the cost that it requires in and of itself. I'm arguing here that it costs more for the IT layer to run than it does for the Data Science layer. And the business value of the layer itself rises as you go up the pyramid. But each layer relies on the layers beneath it. So, you can't really cut out layers.

AI built on data that is not available obviously can't occur.

AI built on data that is not good data is pointless because garbage in leads to garbage out.

Each layer in the diagram requires a different skillset. And whenever you have scale, you have the overhead of management, workflow and procedures. And whenever you have stakeholders, you need people who can elicit requirements. And when you have smart people thinking about the process and systems that they use, you get multiple approaches and policies that generate new roles and new skills requirements.

So, there are a lot of different jobs with a lot of different skills. And that's before you even start to consider the different *flavours* of analytics.

I define flavours of analytics as being the sort of things that would be mentioned in job advertisements. Examples include:

- Digital analytics for web and ecommerce.
- Operations analytics for monitoring manufacturing processes.
- Supply chain analytics monitoring the geographic location of a firm's goods.
- Commercial analytics covering what is sold where.
- Financial crime analytics ranging from monitoring the real time transactions on credit cards, all the way through to analysing digital documents.

Each flavour of analytics has its own three letter acronyms, its own assumptions and standard analyses that are performing thousands of times. They have their own niche tools, their own challenges and opportunities. They have their own awards, conferences, and podcasts.

And it's important to understand some of these differences and assumptions so that you know, for example, a digital analyst is most likely to have to deal with data about web traffic and ecommerce. They might be asked about user journeys, A/B testing of different UX or UI. The metric to optimise might be basket size or sales. The key tools they might be expected to know could include Adobe Analytics or Google Analytics.

However, an e-discovery analyst might be expected to know how to use Relativity and may be asked to consume millions of emails and thousands of printed documents, while looking for particular terms and phrases.

You will definitely need to know this when you apply for jobs, because unless you promote yourself as a generalist, it is easier to obtain promotions and advancement if you develop an in-depth knowledge of one area of analytics.

So, while the breadth of roles and types of analytics is huge, I will boil down the advice I give in this book to the commonality of analytics as an industry. To summarise; analytics generates value by turning data into insights.

I will point out: I have added the measurement of Business Value, the estimation of Cost and the example of job title to each of the layers in the Hierarchy of Needs - and some people may disagree with those additions. But I've done that to ensure that I can tease out another point I want to make about analytics and the roles within it:

I consider data engineering to be a subset of analytics. I consider data science to be a subset of analytics. But I do not consider the IT functions of data collection to be part of analytics. I'll talk about that in a later chapter.

PART 2

Measuring Analytics

It's hilarious to me that, for an industry that prides itself on recommending changes to business processes and activities based on measuring some part of the business, measuring analytics itself is so problematic.

Why do we need to measure analytics? It's important from a career perspective to be aware of the opportunities and challenges that come with a job. By gauging where the business and the analytics function are in terms of maturity, we can best match our aspirations with the reality of what the work environment is likely to be. If you aspire to do AI there is little point in taking a job in which the movement of data still relies on numerous Excel spreadsheets emailed between analysts. It's still possible to do AI, but you might want to find a job with a more sophisticated data environment.

Likewise, if there is a toxic political situation at senior manager level, are you going to be able to thrive?

This section of the book identifies the areas you should ask about to obtain the full picture of an analytics function. From there you can be fully informed to support your career decisions.

CHAPTER 2

Internal Relationships

There are three relationships within analytics: the relationship with data, how the analytics work is handled operationally, and the politics of the function. We'll look at each of these in turn.

Data

There are a lot of people thinking about data. They write and share their thoughts, and movements have been formed around the more influential of the concepts. You've probably heard of them – concepts like Data Warehouses, Data Lakes, Data Lakehouses, Data Swamps, Data Mesh, Data Contracts, Data Products, Data as a Service, etc.

But when I think of an analytics organisation's relationship with data, I ignore those labels and look at the practical attitudes of the function and how they handle the following four aspects of data: Automation, Monitoring, Providence and Legal/Governance.

Automation

Very immature analytics functions do not automate anything. They have spreadsheets in which data is copied and pasted manually, and processes that grind to a halt if someone forgets to close a file on a shared drive.

This is bad on many levels: if someone is away or the process is not documented then the outputs of the process are in jeopardy. This situation is not an indication of the intelligence of the people within the function: environments like this usually occur because the technology available to the team is limited and the team must get by with what they've got. The processes grow and develop organically as additional requirements are added over the months and years, while the systems do not grow more sophisticated in parallel.

A level of maturity is possible when an organisation has leadership who obtain a budget for a tool to store and move their data around.

Managing the flood of automations is the next challenge that establishes the maturity level of the function's relationship with Data. Having controls over which dataflows are automated and the process whereby they are automated is the next level of maturity – and in a lot of cases is driven by cost considerations. When you have a huge bill for cloud processing and storage, it makes you think a little harder about the kind of things you want running in the cloud and how much data you want to store.

So, if I had to categorise how I measure automation, I'd tend to give it one of three scores: *immature* where there is no automation, *some maturity* where there are no controls over what is automated and *mature* where there are checks and balances put in place.

Monitoring

Automation removes people from the process of moving data from source systems to a place where it can be used. But one of the few positives in having people involved in the manual process is that there are more pairs of eyes on the data, and therefore it is more likely that someone will notice errors or mistakes before they infect the end result.

Monitoring encompasses the steps taken to ensure that the data processed is correct. In a perfect world this step is not required. Data flows operate uninterrupted. Disks never run out of space. Dependent flows always kick off when the data is available. But we don't live in a perfect world. Things go wrong, and Monitoring is the only way of ensuring that the errors introduced by events going wrong don't infect your outputs.

Monitoring includes Data Quality.

> Data quality is a measure of the condition of data based on factors such as accuracy, completeness, consistency, reliability and whether it's up to date.[3]

It includes anomaly detection and therefore requires a sense of what an acceptable range of values is for each metric. As a result, measuring how well analytics does Monitoring is also a good indication of how well analytics knows and understands the data from a business point of view.

Providence

Being able to trace where data comes from, what processes move it, where it is used and who consumes it is important for a number of reasons, not least of which are assisting in fault finding and importantly, establishing the audience for delay notifications.

Story time

I worked somewhere where there was a large team of analysts who were operating without a lot of management supervision. More

---

[3]https://www.techtarget.com/searchdatamanagement/definition/data-quality

importantly, there were no guidelines concerning the generation of data workloads, and as a result they were awash with workflows. Some of these were still being run despite having been superseded by subsequent versions of the flow, others were broken and yet more were only being run manually. A similar situation was in place with the front-end dashboards. Users were complaining of their dashboards being moved when their bookmarks didn't work anymore. There were also complaints about the data being stale and not being told that there were issues with the data.

A pretty dire situation.

The good news was that I had a strong technical knowledge of the two tools we used for ETL (Alteryx) and dashboarding (Tableau). Tableau is a drag-and-drop dashboarding tool that has an API allowing access to a lot of the metadata. Alteryx is a drag-and-drop ETL tool that stores its metadata as xml. The great thing about Alteryx is that you can point it at a folder and get it to parse XML files. So, I set up a flow that read all the org's Alteryx workflows and pulled out the Input and Output nodes. As their names suggest, these are the parts of the workflows that identify where the data comes from and where it ends up. My flow also indicated the last time the workflow was run and when it was completed successfully. This generated a picture of where the data was going and which workflows were sending it, where there were multiple workflows dealing with the same data and which flows were kicking off but never finishing successfully. Very valuable data.

Likewise, getting a picture of the data sources for all the Tableau dashboards was straightforward using the Tableau API. So, I could obtain all the data sources for each of the dashboards, as well as the usage data, including who was accessing the dashboards and how frequently. Again, Alteryx interacted with APIs so I could also use those skills to generate that data.

Now, once you have both sets of data – where the data comes from, where it goes, plus the usages of that data – you can generate a visualisation of the flow of data for the entire org. This is an incredibly powerful tool. It allows you to trace bugs and problematic data upstream to where they're originating. Was it the data at source or was a workflow introducing an incorrect aggregation? Was there more than one workflow moving the data and the first one was an old version with logic that has subsequently been changed? It allows you to tell the right people about delays in data or give warnings about future delays. It also allows you to be comfortable with the scope of the work that the team is doing. Importantly, it very quickly answers questions like, "If we change the data source for this type of data, what areas of the business will be affected?" and, "Who uses our dashboards?"

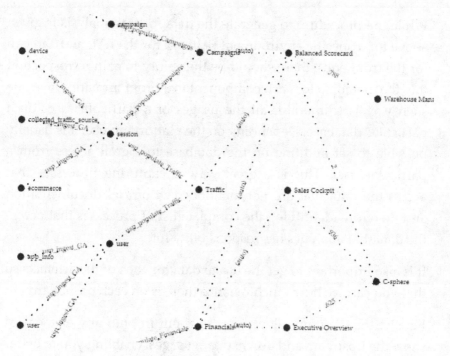

Figure 3 Data flow (source to usage)

The goal was to generate a network diagram like figure 3 (this is an extremely simplified version for the sake of illustration. The original diagram had over two thousand processes and hundreds of tables, and when printed took up a couple of A0 sized pieces of paper). From left to right we look at:

- The external sources of the data.
- The internal tables in which the external data is ingested.
- The internal translations, whether instantiated or logical.
- The layer of data presented to the visualisation layer.
- The dashboard or other artefacts used to expose the data to the users.
- Finally, the user groups who consume the different dashboards or other artefacts.

While the procedure to generate the data for this analysis is given above for a specific environment (Alteryx for the ETL and Tableau for the front end), there should be the ability to gain introspection into the metadata for each component in a programmatic way. One such way is to monitor all the usages of a particular user on a particular database. Depending on the platform in use, it is usually possible to set auditing on the database to log all access from a particular user. This is a great way of capturing processes that access the data that are not mentioned in official documentation and therefore identifying the complete list of processes that access the data that analytics has responsibility for.

It is also important to get the usage data for each of the artefacts so that you can see how much reliance there is on each dashboard.

Finally, the diagram allows you to zoom in onto any element to show the upstream and downstream usages, enabling you to better identify bugs.

It is important to either filter out the developers of the dashboards from the usage stats, or else include the developers as a user group so that you can remove the inevitable spike in usage by the developers during development Having a separate development environment is also helpful in this regard, but you'll always have user acceptance testing, which might have a usage inflationary effect.

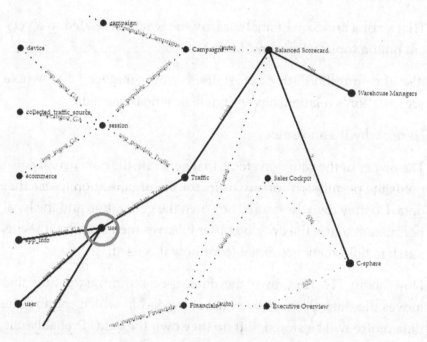

Figure 4 Data flow (source to usage) – one flow highlighted.

Legal/Governance

Finally, the Data Protection Act 2018 represents the UK's implementation of the General Data Protection Regulation (GDPR). Jurisdictions all over the world have similar legislations that boil down to this: make sure you have the permissions to use personal data for the usages that you require, and make sure that your storage of that data meets the legal requirements of the different countries in which you operate.

In my experience, analytics is not the department that drives compliance with this legal requirement. Instead, Legal or Risk departments get in touch with the analytics department and let them know that they need to comply. Analytics' relationship with data is more about consuming as much of the data available in order to future-proof the department from requests for analytics in the future.

That's not a criticism of analytics, by the way! It's related to a very hot button topic: who owns data?

It's the question that crystalises how mature the whole organisation's relationship with data is: who owns data?

Here's why it's an issue:

The owner of the source systems that generate the data usually also holds the permissions of any users for the organisation to use that data. Do they own the data? They own the generation and the legal permission to use the data, but after it leaves their systems it seems harsh to hold them accountable for how it is used.

How about IT? They own the databases, the infrastructure that moves the data, perhaps even have decided in which country the data centre will be stored. But do they own the data? Probably not.

What about analytics? They move the data, they use the data, they copy the data. They breach the law if they use the data for purposes not covered by user permissions. Do they own the data? Maybe.

What about the business? The people who want the data interrogated? They are looking for the insights that they need to do their jobs and to generate income. They obviously do not own the data.

If analytics doesn't step up and take responsibility for the data, then they are potentially going to be breaking the law by doing their jobs. If the Sales team want a list of people to contact and that data was only collected under the express condition that it was not used for any sales purpose, then by fulfilling that request analytics is breaking the law. So, if for no other reason than self-preservation, it makes sense for analytics to not only collect, manipulate and store the data, but also to collect the permissions and know how the data can be used.

After asking who owns the data, I usually ask when they dispose of data. It's possible for an analytics org to proudly state that they own the data, that they have a good handle on what they are allowed to do with the data, and then look rather blankly at me when I ask them when they get rid of data.

A big part of the data governance area is how much thought is given to the retention – and more importantly the deletion – of data. A lot of the places I have worked have not considered data deletion, primarily because they were focussing on the operational uses of data rather than their role as custodians or owners of the data. However, any well-run data organisation considers not only the sourcing of data, proving provenance and the flows that transform and move the data from environment to environment, but also the permissions, the length of time that they want to retain the data and the process and mechanisms for deleting the data.

Operational

It has been my experience that as teams get larger, the spread of abilities within the team increases. An attempt by management to harness the team's efforts and deliver business value is captured in the inevitable chosen system of workflow management. This is because not everyone in your team may have the same conscientious approach to undertaking work and reporting their progress, so you "need" a workflow management tool. I suspect that it is also how middle management justify their position. It certainly makes it easier to report on progress and sum up the output of the team. In the best case, this is a light touch way for management and stakeholders to know who is dealing with which tasks and how much progress has been made on them. Alternatively, it can also be an exercise in bureaucracy.

When scoring the relationship that analytics has with operational processes, consider how much time you spend talking about work rather than actually doing it. This overhead is usually borne by the people doing the work and so a system implemented with good intentions by management might be having a disproportionate impact on the team's total number of work hours.

The relationship of the analytics organisation with data and its relationship with operational processes are linked to the culture that the analytics org wants to set, and influence the priorities that are seen as important. It's incredibly easy for senior management to say things like, "The accuracy of our data is important," but what are they doing to make sure that is the case? A good answer would be something like, "As our standard operating procedure, we check the checksum of all of our datasets against the source system." For the evaluation of operational processes, some questions to consider include:

- Do we carve out time to retire code?
- Do we refactor code to address bugs before they become an issue?
- How many layers of review occur before releasing into production?
- Is all the code stored centrally?
- Is there any provision for work that analytics wants to do that has not been asked for?
- How many person hours do we spend on our operational processes?
- On documentation?
- On filling in time and motion surveys?
- On updating Jira boards?
- On estimating and planning sprints?

One of the biggest questions I have for organisations is:

What are the connections between the operational processes and how individuals are judged and rewarded?

My issue with workflow products is that it focuses on measuring the outputs rather than the outcomes and turns the focus of the analytic department's middle management inward. They measure the number of tickets or projects delivered, instead of the outcomes of those projects. It's very easy for managers to advertise a 15% increase in resolving tickets. It's much harder to point out a metric that moves the needle for the business as a whole, or the department that they support. It's not all analytics' fault though; frequently the recommendations made by analytics, whether as a result of answering business questions or not, are not acted upon. If they are, the maths on whether they had an impact is messy and therefore it's hard to tease out exactly how much effect those recommendations had. It's hard to attribute an increase in sales to the recommendations made by analytics when there are many contributing factors to changes in sales.

Politics

Who are the favourites? Who does senior management talk to? What is the strategic direction of the function?

Identifying the posturing and manoeuvring of senior management can be difficult as these are things that usually occur behind closed doors. But you can sometimes piece together a view of the relationships between different levels of senior management. Why is this important?

I worked in an org where the head of analytics was having a significant disagreement with her boss regarding who would be responsible for implementing changes based on the results of analytics. This was a contentious issue.

Typically, a business function finances a number of analysts to support their part of the business. The business unit decides what insights they need, and the analysts work to provide those insights. The business unit then decides how to operationalise those insights and what actions should be taken as a result of them.

Frequently there will be a vague statement made about how the business unit wants analytics to be a "trusted partner" and that analytics should know the business so well that they should be suggesting insights that will support the business unit's goals and objectives.

That is good practice. But in this case, the head of analytics was getting frustrated that the stakeholders were not implementing the results of her team's analyses. And so, she wanted to shift the locus of change from the business to her team, which ignited a lot of conflict regarding who should be driving the change in the business.

It's always made sense to me that analytics provides the ammunition for the business unit to deliver the change. However, if the stated goal is for analytics to be the trusted business partner of the business unit that it supports, and the proof of that relationship is the presentation of ideas and actions that (a) the business unit has not asked for and which (b) show that the analytics resource knows the business better than the business unit themselves, then the next most obvious step is for the analytics resource to actually run the business unit. But as soon as this line is crossed we have muddied the water of what the business unit is, and what comprises analytics.

Provocative idea: there is an argument that analytics should not exist as a separate entity, and that it merely represents a skill that should be common across the business as a whole. Until analytics skills are much more common I think we're safe in our specialisation, but it is important to note that there is a natural limit to the work that we can do in analytics. Figuring out where the borders are – early – is a good political move.

Why didn't I include this anecdote in the section on External Relationships, specifically the section on Stakeholder relationships? Think about what you would do if you were a manager or an IC in the analytics department where your boss or boss' boss was making arguments that analytics should be driving the change to the business, rather than your stakeholders. How would that realisation change your conversations with those stakeholders? With your boss?

Knowing the internal politics within the analytics department – what goes on behind closed doors – is essential in judging and measuring that analytics department.

CHAPTER 3

External Relationships

Thinking about our definition of analytics, the two primary external relationships could be described as upstream and downstream. Upstream is IT, because most of the time that it is who analytics have to talk to in order to get access to data. And downstream are the stakeholders, because they consume the data.

IT

Differences between IT and Analytics

IT and analytics are very different. It's tempting to treat them as the same because they share similar tools and skills, but for the reasons I will explain in this chapter, they are too different to do so. Hopefully these tales from the trenches will highlight the differences.

Story Time I

The simplest story about IT and analytics occurred at a large retail firm I worked at. They had a large online product generation system and both a physical sales network as well as a sizeable e-commerce site. As you can imagine, the volume of data that they had was immense. Website traffic, in-store sales, pricing, stock movements, stock availability, loyalty card transactions, etc. – a lot of data. The analytics function didn't want to have to wait for IT to have resources available and put together a solution that might not match what analytics had in mind, so they put together their own solution. There was enough experience within the function to put together a Proof of Concept – which was also the final product. They arranged all the ETL processes, bringing the data in from the various sources. They documented the columns with good discussion on how they were modified as part of the ingestion. And the senior management had sufficient budgetary discretion to be able to do it all at a scale that supported the complete analytics function.

When it was up and running and all the analysts across the org were using it in anger, generating insights and answering the business questions, only then did analytics approach IT to arrange support. IT then identified where there was an internal skills deficiency and hired the necessary people to support those systems.

The only reason this actually worked was because the IT team was mature enough to accept that they hadn't been involved with the build, then they swallowed their pride and took it on to run it. They hadn't been asked to create it because they didn't have the skill set. And with my experience in other orgs, I can say that if analytics had waited for IT, the project probably would not have worked. This is also an example of political capital – whoever was running analytics and decided to go ahead with the project had to have enough staff with the right skills and the right budget to get it off the ground. And I suspect that if IT got wind of the efforts, then the analytics managers would have to have high enough political capital to stave off challenges that argued IT should be doing the work. An argument that analytics may have used here is that there was more business value to be unlocked by getting things up and running themselves, rather than waiting for IT to prioritise the project and run it through their backlog grooming, specifying the requirements and resourcing and funding the project from scratch. There's a never-ending list of projects for IT and you don't want the analytics org to be waiting for access to data.

Story Time II

I was tasked with getting a new data stream made available to the analytics team for my employer. So, I had to talk to IT about getting the data required for the analysis. I filled in their form for the business case and then sat down with a BA to go through the documentation.

"You say you need all the data from this stream, what's the business requirement for that much data?"

"We need to be able to report on the performance of that process, so we need to have the data."

"So, who will use that data?"

"The management of that process will look at the dashboards that we build so that they can change what they're doing and save money or increase revenue by focusing on the bits that are working."

"So, it sounds like you don't actually need every one of these columns."

"Sure, but we don't know the exact analyses that we will be required to perform now, and it takes six months to get IT resources to make changes, so we need to have access to them all."

"We'd really like for you to reduce the scope of what you're asking for so that we're not storing data that we don't need to."

I spent an increasingly frustrating time going back and forth between IT and the business stakeholder, negotiating to try to maximise the data we would have available while not being able to prove business value because the business did not know the reporting that would be required in the future.

The cause of the conflict between the two of us was that IT was operating under a paradigm that sought to:

- Create functionality – ship features.
- Limit Scope – focus on the minimum requirements to ensure no waste of resource, no wastage in terms of storage costs and to allow adding the resource required into their resource plan.

Whereas analytics were operating under a paradigm of

- Create capability – the ability to provide multiple insights to multiple stakeholders.
- Operate around long lead times for IT resource.
- The cost of storing the data was a sunk cost from our perspective.

I'd love to say that I got the result I needed, but I didn't. From my point of view IT was unhelpful. From their point of view, I was inexact and overreaching with my requirements.

What I should have done was to find out why IT was so keen to restrict the data. I suspect it was because the data centre that we used was on Prem, using an expensive solution that was supposed to be turned off within two years. But there was no cloud alternative on the cards because the transition to the cloud was a year away. As the holder of the company purse strings, IT thought that they were operating responsibly, but it reminded me of the John A. Shedd quote, "A ship is safe in harbour, but that's not what ships are for." You can't generate business value from insights if you don't have any data. Even if I knew for sure that the cost pressures were preventing the project from going ahead, that knowledge would not have been enough to get the project over the line. In that company there was no cross-charging, so even if I could go up the chain of command and get approval for the expense to come out of someone else's P&L, from IT's point of view it was all cost with no benefit. Without a specific use case that would generate the business value, or a way of specifying an actual business value, the project languished. At that particular company there was also a power vacuum within analytics at the senior leadership level, so there was no support or possibility to apply pressure from senior management.

I bring this up for two reasons: the first is that IT and analytics are very different beasts and are driven by different mindsets and goals. Treating them the same because they use some of the same tools and skills is dangerous.

Secondly, sometimes there is no good answer. Sometimes you have to know when you are wasting your time. It's hard to get this right because you have to be able to defend your position to both analytics senior management as well as the stakeholders expecting you to deliver.

In this case, all I could do was keep my boss informed of my difficulties and to let the stakeholders know that IT was the road block, and request they bring pressure to bear to get the desired result. I had no political capital; my boss had no political capital and what little political capital the stakeholders had they were not willing to spend on this project – even though they were the beneficiaries of it.

Was it a failure on my part to get this project over the line? Arguably.

A Better Story

My team was supporting a monitoring function – the org had regulations that meant some aspect of the business had to be inspected periodically and the results of those inspections had to be stored in a secure system. The original manager of the system was old school IT in the same manner mentioned in the previous story. In fact, he went even further and said there would be no release of the data from his system for the purposes of reporting.

As you can imagine, this made my team's job very difficult. With no data available, the reporting function was starved. In the end (and I must admit that this happened before my time), the manager with responsibility for that system had to be fired because he was preventing the management of the inspection function from knowing how well they were doing against targets, progress and plan out their workload. They could not report on their position to the regulators.

So, only after analytics had the IT manager removed were we allowed access. We had a monthly feed of data. One of my first jobs was to arrange more frequent access. My boss said, "On XX date at XX time, you are going to have a conversation with one of the IT technical team and your goal is to get them to agree to allowing more frequent access." As an aside, this is an awesome way of giving someone a task: don't tell someone how to do it; give them the goal and the autonomy to act and let them get on with it.

The time of the conversation arrived, I got my notepad out to take notes and settled into the open-plan office to jump on the call and get the result I was looking for.

The first topic: why we needed the data. That was easy (see above). We needed to report on it. And there were serious repercussions in a multitude of jurisdictions if we couldn't manage that correctly. So, they were on board there.

"So, why do you need this more than monthly?"

This needed a little more discussion, but the argument I provided was that we needed to make more granular adjustments than could be made monthly, we needed to reflect the efforts of those parts of the org that were making changes to the things we were monitoring, and for that we needed daily updates. As I put it to the appreciation of those sitting around me in the office who couldn't help themselves from listening in. "If I'm driving a car I can't afford to only look out the window once a month, I'll come off the road. I need to take more frequent looks at where I'm going."

And those arguments worked. They replied:

"Yeah, it looks like you need the data, and you need it more often. But we still can't give it to you."

"And why is that?"

"It takes about an hour for the data to be extracted. We are a global business. Therefore, the system has to support staff in Europe, The Americas and in Asia, in the Pacific as well as India. There is no slot that allows everyone to use the system unaffected."

I asked an important question. "Do we have to support people working outside of their normal workday?"

"No, that would be unreasonable. People know they can only expect it to be up from 9am to 5pm local time."

I quickly sketched out the different time zones involved and the time difference between each of them. "Actually, there is a slot that is available – there's an hour here that allows for your hour of extraction time without affecting anyone's 9-5."

"Great," they said. "I guess we're in business. But we can't let you access the data from the live system. It's against IT policy. You could be reading from a table that is being written to at the same time, causing deadlocks and hanging systems and chaos."

Sigh. "OK, tell me more about the system you've got. Do you do daily backups of the system?"

"Of course, we do, we're a well-run global IT team and we do the needful, but you can't access the daily backups because we need to have those unchanged so we can restore them if needed."

"Yes, that does make sense. Do you have a failover system if there is a power outage or system failure?"

"Yes, we have a secondary system that is mirrored on an hour delay from primary."

"So, the database gets backed up and restored into secondary within an hour? I thought you said it takes at least an hour to get the extract and it must take a while to restore from that backup – how does that work?"

"No, the transaction logs: the individual deletes, inserts and update activity that affects the primary database is also sent to the secondary system and that secondary database is updated within an hour of the original. So, the same change from the front-end interface makes the changes to the primary database and then also sends those changes to the secondary database."

Brainwave! "Is there any policy that says we can't use that one-hour window, when no one is expected to be using the system, to extract the database from the *secondary* system?"

"Let me check... no."

So, we did that. I did not mention that all four time zones had a form of daylight savings that kicked in on different dates, so therefore that one hour slot might exist for some parts of the year and in fact might be two hours sometimes and might not exist at all on other days of the year. I don't think that actually mattered in the end because the extraction was running off the secondary system and so therefore should only have had an impact should there be a catastrophic system failure. There was also value in extracting the data periodically as yet another checkpoint that they could roll back to if needed. It felt good to get that over the line.

The difference between the two IT departments in these stories is that the first one saw analytics as a *customer* (we deliver a solution), the second saw us as a *partner* (we help you do a thing). You always want to use the language of partnership, utilising words like enable, support, and collaborate. In an ideal world you want to have a dedicated resource rather than a project-based resource that has to be booked in advance. It's one thing to negotiate among your analytics powers to release resources and a totally different proposition to try to get resources released from a project where those responsible for delivery are in a different department entirely. With dedicated resources, your analytical requirements will be a steady stream of tasks and having a resourcing model to support that will mean you can react to the changing environment much quicker. The alternative to this is that when the current analytics project is finished you get no follow up support and if there are wrinkles to iron out from data ingestion (which there always are – it's impossible to specify absolutely everything) then you will lose the support you need to deliver the project to 100% completion.

Another Story

Another example of this occurred in an enterprise level organisation where there were so many sources of data and so many analysts creating their own pipelines that it was difficult to keep on top of them all. One of the data engineering practices we used was to have the last step in an ETL process be a quick write to a database table indicating that, "this table has been updated with data for this particular day." Then everyone else could be sure that they had today's data and there were even tools that would allow you to kick off your ETL process but wait until a particular table had been updated before continuing to run the rest of the ETL flow. Great, right? Yes, but there was a part of the business, a subsidiary, who refused to use this practice. There were politics involved and the subsidiary simply refused to share their data at all. If they were ever challenged or asked to do something they didn't want to do, they would refuse point blank and sometimes revoke everyone's access to their data entirely. Those discussions happened well and truly above my paygrade, so I left that alone, but I noticed that more and more of the work my team did was being adversely affected by these tables when we couldn't tell how up-to-date the data was. As a work around, some of the team started polling the tables in question until they found the right date, but that was not very efficient and wasted server resources. It was a widely known issue that everyone wanted fixed – but they threw their hands up and said, "the subsidiary doesn't do it, what are we supposed to do?"

So, I decided that I would have a look at getting this changed. The subsidiary needed to follow our standard practice. It was a non-negotiable practice for the engineering teams everywhere else. So, I reached out to the team leader of the team involved. But not with "Why You No Use Practise?"[4] as the meeting heading, oh no. Softly, softly! I asked to have a chat because we were both analytics managers and I was new in the role (honestly, I'd been in the role for six months at that point in time, so I employed a little white lie) and I just wanted to know about him and his team.

---

[4]https://knowyourmeme.com/memes/y-u-no-guy

Things that I learned: super under resourced, strategic push to increase resourcing in data, but huge backlog. No interest in taking on the practice. They used a different ETL tool than the rest of the org. There were only about two dozen workflows that moved the data over from the subsidiary to our data warehouse. And most importantly: it was possible to add the simple insert that we required to the end of the workflow to indicate that it had successfully run. I even ensured that there was a user account on their side that had access to make the insert into the right table on our side.

"We need to put the practice on those 25 workflows, but it doesn't sound like you can do it," I told him.

"It's task number three hundred in a list of three hundred items. If no other work comes in for two years, then we'll get to it at the end of those two years," he replied.

I nodded as I continued. "But I don't necessarily want you to do it, I just want it done. If I can find a resource using your ETL tool to add that little bit of code to the end of each of those twenty-five ETL workflows, will you give us your blessing to make the changes?"

"Well, we would have to do a code review to make sure we're happy with that."

"Of course! Who is your senior tech person? Who do we need to book time with? Can you clear that with them? Who is their manager?"

I jumped on another call with our IT liaison. Unlike the previous two stories, at this org we *did* have a partnership relationship with IT, and we had dedicated resources. Analytics as a function fought over those resources internally because we all had things we wanted them to do, but there was dedicated support there. I checked with the liaison that our dedicated resources had the right skills and to see if the liaison agreed this was a high priority. They did, and it was. I then reached out to the head of analytics to make sure that they were on board with it too, because it involved reallocating the existing resource from existing projects. I got the ok there and then confirmed the timeline that the IT people could do it in. I then introduced the senior on the subsidiary side to the liaison and set expectations on when we would need their time for the review.

If this was a puff piece, I would say that the whole org carried me aloft on their shoulders and I was feted for my successful result, but it's a real story. So, I got maybe a begrudging nod of approval at best. There are a few things that I could have done to maximise the impact of my success: a roadshow outlining how this helped our data situation with invites to the wider data community, plus the rest of the analytics org. Perhaps going out of my way to praise the cooperation of the subsidiary's IT team to their senior management. What I really should have done was gone to my stakeholders and consumers of the dashboards created using the data and explained that the improvement in availability and timeliness of data was due to the changes we were making and giving shoutouts to both the subsidiary IT team as well as our data IT team. We'll discuss this further in the Guidance section for IC.

Stakeholders

I've left this section towards the end of the chapter but I think it's probably the most important as the relationships you have with problematic stakeholders can very quickly make or break your career.

Stakeholders are those representatives from the business who provide the genesis of analytics work. At most of the places I've worked the funding model has been this:

A part of the business identifies that there is an analytics requirement and provides a business case to pay for the headcount of the analysts. The analysts are then hired and work on those analyses for that part of the business. There may be a team of analysts that support that business unit or there may be one analyst supporting many business units. It's frequently a many-to-many relationship. And there is very seldom a lack of analytics work to be done!

An Aside

If you do find yourself in a tug of war with two or more stakeholders, the danger is that you will be the bad guy as you will have each stakeholder talking to you and asking for support for particular projects, and you will have to tell them no, because you are full up. That very rarely results in a good outcome because they will only see you saying no and will not appreciate all the other things that you are being asked to do. To combat this, get all the stakeholders with claims on your time to attend a planning meeting together. Go through the process of discussing how much time is available for that period and how big each of the projects are.

I've actually been in this position and after explaining the relative size of each of the projects and the team's capacity, I then told the stakeholders that I was going to leave the room and come back in ten minutes – and they were going to discuss the relative merits of each of the projects and then tell me which of these I would be doing. Whenever I did this, I expected to open the door to see the walls covered in blood and one or both of the stakeholders looking up from a full-on fist fight, but that hasn't happened... yet. On this occasion I needed to give them a little more time for the discussion, but twenty minutes later they had come to an agreement, and I was no longer the bad guy. They had all been in the meeting and could trade off their projects and promises of which ones would be done when. So, the big question: why did I leave them to do it in private? In this case it was make it clear that I was not the bottleneck: I was not the one saying no. It was also to allow them to speak frankly to their peers without someone from a different department listening in on their discussions. I could have stayed and tried to arbitrate the discussion, and I think that would have been defensible, but I was worried that it could have been seen as me creating chaos and then revelling in it, rather than just trying to get the right result.

Keep an eye on these situations, as you want to corral the frustration and point it in the right direction – which is the concerted effort from both or all stakeholders who would otherwise fight for your time, to promote to their bosses the idea that more analytics resources are required. If people are told via multiple sources that there is a growing demand for support but a lack of resources to deliver it, then they are more likely to release the purse strings. I have never worked anywhere where there was more analytics resource than there was analytics work. So, there will always be a backlog and prioritisation required.

Sometimes it can be impossible to get both stakeholders in the same room at the same time. This is when you need to be very clear about what the ramifications of missing – or failing to send a delegate to – that meeting would be. You must explain that this meeting, and only this meeting, will be when the allocation of analytics resources will occur for the next period, and should they miss it (or fail to send a delegate) then they are giving up their claim on analytics time. I'd advise copying in their boss so that they're aware. That might get their attention.

Where were we?

Stakeholders themselves are different people with different personalities, behaviours and attitudes, all of which shape their half of the relationship with analytics. When you are trying to establish the strength of the stakeholder relationship, you're looking for clues in the way that people talk about the stakeholders, and how they describe those relationships.

For example, if you are interviewing at a firm and ask about the stakeholders and your potential boss says something like "Oh, yes. Rohit is awesome, we have a great relationship with them, now." You can ask questions about what the relationship was like historically and how it has changed and the type of behaviours that reflect that change in the relationship. This will give you a much better insight into the work environment and more importantly, the power dynamics at play.

Relationships

There are many ways in which a relationship with a stakeholder can be less than desired, and so when you think about identifying problematic stakeholder relationships, you should be specific about what causes you to consider the relationship problematic.

Most of the issues I have seen with problematic stakeholder relationships boil down to what is considered "reasonable." Unfortunately, there are an enormous number of stories about problematic or unreasonable stakeholders. It's important to remember is that the stakeholder doesn't usually set out to be objectionable. Usually. When you discover the stakeholder who makes no bones about the fact that they have put the parameters of reasonable behaviour to one side, congratulations. Either your manager will step up and manage the situation, or else they won't and your work life will be so bad that you will probably have to leave and find a new one. So, congratulations on your new job, or congratulations, your manager is good at their job.

Story Time

I heard about a stakeholder who was supposed to be the interface between a larger stakeholder team and analytics, so they were supposed to give the requirements for dashboards and sign off their acceptance when the dashboards were delivered. Being the representative of their wider team was a Big Deal. The way that promotions worked in that company was that it was easier to get one if you could illustrate that you were "taking responsibility" for something. What that "taking responsibility" actually entailed was never quite spelled out, so you had a lot of managers running around claiming that they were "taking responsibility" in preparation for their promotion business case but not actually doing anything to reflect that claim.

In our case this individual would give the analytics team the requirements, the team would build the dashboards and then the individual would sign them off. So far, so good, right? The problem started when one of the stakeholder's wider team would complain about a part of the dashboard – a filter that they decided was required, or a field that needed to be there but wasn't included – that sort of thing. The stakeholder would come to us and say that we hadn't done it right, despite this new requirement not being mentioned in the scoping phase. The phrase, "you should have known about it," was frequently used.

We tried to get around this terrible state of affairs by asking to have a wider audience for scoping, so that we could get these additional requirements, but were told that the stakeholder was the only person we could talk to. Unfortunately, we did not have sufficient cover from a senior management point of view, so this was a situation that persisted.

To say that this stakeholder relationship left a lot to be desired would be an understatement.

CHAPTER 4

ROI

Return on investment (ROI) is a financial planning strategy for determining the value of a project to predict how it may perform. Accurately calculating ROI can help organizations make the right investments.[5]

Very frequently a person in analytics will be asked by someone what the ROI is of a proposed piece of work. This chapter will seek to discuss this matter and give you some ammunition for answering such a question. This chapter is in the section about Measuring Analytics because what could be more "Measuring Analytics" than trying to calculate the value and cost of a piece of work?

Analytics doesn't produce anything.[6]

I was chatting with Peter O'Neill of MeasureCamp[7] fame when he came up with that provocative statement. And after teasing out what he meant, I agree with him. Let me explain.

Let's talk about front line revenue departments. The sales teams, the business development folk. They produce sales. You can measure their success in monetary terms. Their efforts are so directly linked

---

[5]https://www.indeed.com/career-advice/career-development/project-roi
[6]https://www.linkedin.com/in/peteroneill/
[7]https://www.measurecamp.org/

to revenue that their compensation is frequently connected to their success.

Now let's talk about those employees working in supply chain. The warehouse folk, the people in Shipping. They make sure there is stock on the shelves so that customers can buy the goods.

Now let's talk about HR. They are brought in to handle sticky situations to protect the company from lawsuits, among other duties. Lawsuits, which could lead to fines or penalties. They reduce avoidable expenses.

Now let's talk about the Legal department. They reduce or avoid fines and legal expenses by addressing legal issues. Again, they're avoiding expenses. They do other things as well, of course, but from an ROI point of view, that's how they justify the cost of their department.

And now let's talk about Analytics. We're not operational – we have no P in the P&L. What do we produce? We don't make widgets. We don't directly ensure that stock is on the shelves. We're not a hygiene factor like HR or Legal or Accounting. What expenses do we reduce? We may make recommendations, but we don't actually make the business change – do we?

In fact, that's one of the sources of frustration for many analytics functions. We get a business question, we understand it, we sit with the business unit and talk about it and then we get the data, crunch the numbers and then present the recommendation back to the business unit who asked the question in the first place. And what do they do? Nothing. If we're lucky they say, "Thanks."

In fact, that lack of action was so bad at one location I worked that halfway through the meeting with the business to discuss the task, the analytics manager would hold up a hand.

"Let's say we answer this question for you. Let's say we build a dashboard and keep it up to date. Let's say we debug the workflow when there is an issue and trace problematic data upstream when we find it. What are you going to do off the back of that work? Off all that maintenance overhead? What changes will you make to what you do?"

In the best-case meetings, the business representatives would say something like, "Well, if there are call centre reps who are in the red zone here, we will start performance managing them. And if they don't move out of the red zone because they are not showing any performance improvement, then we will manage them out of the business." It was the best case because they were taking concrete action from the artefact we produced, and they would be continuing to use the artefact over time. It was worth us delivering the artefact and adding the supporting workflows to the list of things we supported.

In the worst case meeting I attended, the people from the business would look at us uncertainly and say something like, "Well, we just want to know." It's hard to justify the resource expended to produce that recommendation, even if it is a one off with no ongoing support needed. That's not to mention the opportunity cost: what we could have been doing instead.

Actually, the worst-case scenario was when the businesspeople decided that they wouldn't say, "We just want to know," and would instead replace it with, "We will monitor the situation and make the necessary adjustments to the business that emerge as a result of the dashboard." Three months after the delivery of that dashboard we checked the stats. Sure enough, as near to zero as it's possible to get in terms of usage.

So, the point there is that analytics does not directly increase revenue, and it doesn't directly reduce expenses. It enables other people to do their jobs better. And sometimes that has an easily identifiable monetary impact, but in my experience it commonly does not.

This is the crux of my argument. You usually can't measure the ROI of a piece of analytics work because the benefit is filtered through the stakeholder's actions.

"But hang on," you might say. "This whole section of the book is about measuring analytics. How can you say that it's not possible to measure the ROI of analytics if in the same breath you're trying to say that it is possible to measure analytics?"

It's an important distinction to make. On the one hand, I am indeed saying that you can't work out the ROI on analytics work. But I am also saying that it is very possible to work out how well analytics operates. You can definitely give a score for each of the components that I have mentioned: how well analytics looks at data, how well it deals with stakeholders and IT. You can even give different scores for the relationship that each team member has with one particular stakeholder. Because (although all opinion) none of these measurements purports to establish the benefit to the business of the analytic function. And the scores you would give would not be in terms of dollars, but more like "never problematic," "sometimes problematic," "problematic" and "toxic" for relationships.

An Aside

I know that some analytics are an exception here. Some studies lend themselves to an ROI exercise because there is an easily identifiable positive that can be measured alongside the costs. And it annoys me no end when people talking about ROI in an analytics context trot those examples out as if they are the only type of analytics that are used.

Experimentation

Experimentation is the best example of why requiring ROI for analytics is ridiculous. A/B or Multivariate testing is when you split your users into groups and then present them with two different experiences. By holding all other variables the same, you can see which experience produces the outcome that you would prefer.

An example might be the colour of a "Buy" button on an ecommerce website. Half the people see a green button, half see a blue button. A week later you compare the sales of each group. If the blue button does better, then you make everyone see a blue Buy button, if the green does better then everyone sees a green one. Basic stuff.

But what would you say if someone asked what the ROI of that analysis was? Before it is run? The whole point of the experiment is to see what the value of blue versus green is. Asking up front seems to be premature. When you are setting up Experimentation as a function, I would imagine you'd say something like, "We will spend this much on doing experiments that we think will move the needle and after the fact we will see if we have generated enough benefit to justify the costs." Failure to do so is not an argument against experimentation as much an argument about the people or process of that experimentation.

I argue that analytics ROI is like that – it's not possible to do at the analysis level, but instead could be done as an aggregate of all the efforts over the year. There is a backlog of assorted analytics activities to support whichever stakeholder was able to secure the budget. And at the end of the year, it's the stakeholder who has to justify their choice of activities based on the benefits that they were able to generate. But they usually don't have to justify themselves to whoever is asking for an ROI. They are responsible to *their* bosses.

Output vs Outcomes

So how *do* you answer the question about ROI?

Some people measure the value of their analytics org by the number of story points the team gets through in a month or a year. Alternately, they may calculate how many JIRA jobs or tasks or projects that their team gets through. These are all usually metrics that are easy to generate from whatever operational system that they are using to manage the team's workflow. But they are all terrible measures of the value to the business because they are focussing on *output*.

We should be looking at the *outcome* that results from analytics activities. How have we changed the business as a result of the work that we do? And if it's not possible to establish in monetary terms, how can we measure that change? What metrics *should* we be using?

Some people look at how they are changing the Data Maturity of the company. That's not a bad outcome, although perhaps a little difficult to measure and attribute to the analytics team. We'll come to that shortly.

I would argue that one metric that should be included in the mix is *attention*. How embedded in the day-to-day operations of your stakeholder are the artefacts that you generate? If they want 20 dashboards, are they using them all? Do they use them every day? Do they get the data that they need from somewhere else because there is something wrong with the dashboards that you have produced? What are the usage stats on the dashboard that you have spent so much time generating? And here is the crunch metric: what did they do with it?

An Aside

How do I have a hard conversation when the stakeholder (whether a manager or someone on their team) asks for something that I suspect is a waste of time?

Ask them what they will use it for. Ask how often. Tell them that you will measure the usage of the product. And at the end of the year, you will present their manager with a list of everything they asked for personally, the length of time and number of people it took to make it. And most importantly the number of times it was looked at and by whom. And you will do this quarterly so that there are no surprises. You want to be on their side so that everyone wins.

The chances are good that the people who are supposed to be using the dashboard are not the actual stakeholder asking for it. In which case, if you can, block out some time for a debrief after a month or three to go through the results with them and then with the audience who is supposed to be using the artefact.

Did you do a roadshow? Was there training? Were there reminders about the artefact? Did you follow up with the users to see why they are using the artefact? Did you highlight the peers who were using the artefacts the most and those with the lowest usage?

If you're thinking to yourself, "That's not part of my job," talk to your boss: it should be. You should be providing business value. If your boss says that your job is just delivering the artefact then I'm sorry, but regardless of what it says on your business card, you are a report monkey. This is a dead-end job where you are an automaton generating artefacts day in, day out. Without any interest in moving the needle for the business you will be stuck until the boss leaves, or you decide to move on: the value of actually being a thought partner will never be realised.

Or perhaps it will, but the disconnect between work that counts and simply the volume of work will be ignored.

Here's the thing. You are responsible for the allocation of resources on this project. The resource that could be applied to any number of projects. I have never worked anywhere where the analytics teams twiddle their thumbs – there's always way too much to do. If you want to be grandiose about it, you are responsible for the responsible allocation of the company resources to the right projects. You have a responsibility to the shareholders, to the management, and to your team to make sure that only work worthy of being done is even started.

You want the stakeholder to be successful. You don't want them carrying the can. So, if the audience that is supposed to use the dashboard do not use the dashboard, you want to help them find out why so that you can address the issue and your stakeholder looks good. Never set up conversations with your stakeholder that end with, "No, because this idea is bad." Set it up so that you are helping them prove the value of their idea. If they falter and say, "Maybe not," because they rethink their ask, don't be afraid to check in with them as to why. If they're worried about the audience not using it, tell them the things you can try to do to get it embedded. Have they spoken to the management team of the proposed audience? They will definitely need to be onside.

Data Maturity

One idea that emerged in my interviews was the concept of Data Maturity as a measure of success. I was a bit confused because although "data maturity" has long been held up as a general guiding principle, I had never heard of it being used as something you could actually measure. Upon further investigation, it turned out that the manager I was talking to would send out a survey to determine how the business used data and how they wanted to do so in the future. The change over time was an indication of the work that analytics was doing. Now, I was puzzled. That didn't make sense: all the interactions that the stakeholders had regarding data would affect that score, surely? What if one of their stakeholders went on a course or had an epiphany? That would move the needle in terms of maturity. The manager nodded. That was true, but likely to be an isolated event. And so, on aggregate most of the movement in the scores could be attributed to the work that the analytics team was doing. I could appreciate that any change in the data maturity scores on the survey would be a movement in the right direction, but appropriating those changes as being evidence of success didn't sit well with me.

There's a lot of literature available if you want further reading on Data Maturity, complete with models and questionnaires and supporting documentation. But I'd like to share one anecdote.

An example of a business driven by data: TripAdvisor. They split the traffic to the site into 100 slices. 20 of those slices were reserved for the control population. People in those slices were served up the standard site with no experiments. The other eighty slices were assigned to various experiments. Some of the experiments received more traffic than others, so you might have forty experiments, one of them having ten slices, a whole lot just getting one slice and some getting two to five slices each. An experiment could be anything from UI changes to the colour, shape or position of certain buttons, or perhaps a change in the flow between pages on the site.

Once a month the Data Science team would present the results of the experiments and then those successful experiments would be rolled into the standard site. In this way the site would be constantly improving and the experiments that were a favourite of one of the product managers but which did not move the needle with regards to revenue or customer satisfaction would be dropped. It was a great way to remove the ego and focus on what the numbers were demonstrating.

Steve Kaufer, the CEO, was in those meetings and one month when the Data Science team had presented, he frowned and said, "Hang on. Last month you showed the successful experiments, and some of those had a good three or four percent uptick in revenue. And so, we rolled those into the standard site and we're not seeing anywhere near a three percent uptick in revenue. In fact, if the Commercial team is to be believed, we're actually trending downwards slightly. What's going on?"

And it was true. One data team was showing a line going up while the other was showing it going down. The managers of the two analytics teams looked at each other, puzzled. Both of them were certain that their data was correct, but the CEO was right: they showed contradictory pictures of the performance. The Commercial team could refer to the actual income generated, so they had somewhat more solid footing there. Everyone was sent back to their desks to figure out what was happening. And that's when I happened by.

"Why all the long faces?"

They told me, showing me the two A4 printouts of the graphs and how one of the line graphs was slowly sinking while the other had a slightly more upwards movement. "If the experiments are working, why is the revenue going down?"

I looked closely at the charts and shifted the experimental one so it was on a slight angle. The line was now matching the line on the revenue one. The wiggles very closely matched and the light of recognition blazed in their eyes. "It looks to me like the experiments are making things better, and without them the revenue decrease would be even higher. It's just a matter of perspective. The one percent drop would be something like two and a half to three percent without these experiments."

I've never seen a group of people with such contradictory emotions competing on their faces: the relief of being able to explain the difference, but the pain of the bad commercial position being potentially worse than they thought.[8]

Consulting Firms & Agencies

Consulting and Agencies are the only exceptions I can think of for my general rule that you can't work out an ROI for analytics work. These are the only two areas in which there is a very real and measurable revenue component that accompanies the analytics work. However, because of that there are dangers in working for a business in which your contribution to business value is so easily measured.

One of those dangers is an internal one. When you can see that you are working on a big project and you are being charged to the client at £300ph and you are on salary earning £45k, the requirement for working overtime or weekends (again, billable to the client, but no additional benefit to you because you are salaried) takes a slightly different flavour. Sure, you are a valued member of the team and are focussing on getting those deliverables out the door in time for the deadline, but you better be recognised for the work that you are doing, learning new skills or somehow advancing your career in another concrete manner. The danger here is that the transparency

---

[8]OK, this didn't happen *exactly* like I have written it. I wasn't the one pointing out the explanation: the Managers came to the conclusion after about ten minutes themselves.

of the commercial arrangement leaves you feeling dissatisfied with your employment.

The other danger is an operational one. Typically, in Consulting or Agency there are productivity metrics on your work. Very broadly it looks at the percentage of the hours that you are working that can be charged to the client. So, take every hour you're in the office and remove all the training, business development and team admin activities, and what's left are the hours that you're working on client work. That proportion has to be high enough to justify your salary. People are frequently let go from these firms for not having a high enough productivity score, but as these businesses are very competitive, it is not unheard of for even those who clear the published hurdle of that metric to be put through performance management processes. One senior manager told me that when the market dipped, they were told to put their bottom 10% in productivity metrics onto PIPs (Performance Improvement Plans) – regardless of how well they were performing.

How To Answer the ROI Question?

I'm sorry it's taken so long to get to this point. There are a lot of people who think that you can have an ROI in analytics and all the above is to address their concerns and arguments. But what do you actually say when someone asks that dreaded question, "What is the ROI of this piece of work?"

Ooh, that's hard. You see, when someone is asking you for the ROI on a piece of analytics work, two things are happening. The first is that they are positioning themselves as an authority figure: you have to justify yourself to them. The second is that they are setting the rules of engagement. If they ask for an ROI, you are the one who has to estimate the benefit to the business. You have to justify the cost to realise that benefit. And then you have to provide those to the person asking.

The first thing I would do is to repeat back explicitly what they are implying. What is the ramification of not providing this?

"So, you're saying that you won't help me with this data ingestion until I come up with a cost benefit analysis?"

"Yes, that's right."

"Unfortunately, I can't point to a dollar figure coming out of this project. And I won't be able to, as the benefits will be realised over a long period of time by answering questions that are not known at the moment as business value arrives independently from each use case. But I think that we are going to be talking at cross purposes here. Who do you report to?"

You can't talk to them with the implicit acknowledgement of the power dynamic. You should not have to justify yourself to someone else using their metrics when they don't apply – or can't apply. Why do I say that they don't apply? Because you were hired. The fact that you and your team and the whole analytics function were hired means that there is recognition of the value of the work that you will do. You don't have access to that business case, but you are the living breathing evidence that it was enough to justify your headcount and associated cost. And justifying the individual components of the work that each analytics person does, probably needs to happen at the Head of Department level – but that's not a discussion for now. The Head of Department who pays your salary and decides what you do to support their department doesn't need to justify themselves to the person asking this ROI question. So, whoever runs analytics needs to talk to the people that are raising these ROI questions and tell them that it's not possible.

This next point is worth writing down: one of the big reasons for this is that there is no guarantee that the part of the business that you support will follow your recommendations based on the reporting that you are doing, and therefore your "return" on your ROI calculation can't be worked out. Additionally, if you have a pricing task that makes sure that you are pricing correctly, what are the ramifications of getting that right? Or getting it wrong? Or recommending something so the department can get their pricing right but they don't implement it? How can you judge the return in each of these cases?

There will always be exceptions to this rule: cases when there will be an easily calculated return – in that case perhaps it's fine to do the calculations and justify yourself to whoever is asking. But know that somewhere down the line there will be a case in which there are philosophical reasons you shouldn't be playing these games.

So, be polite. But don't play their game.

PART 3

General Guidance

This part of the book will look at non-job specific advice for working in analytics. We will cover some pointers on how to get into analytics, but first we will attempt to identify the major aspects of a job in analytics that will colour your experience. The biggest aspect of the job has to be the country in which you will be working. Another major consideration will be the industry in which your employer operates. A third point that will affect your work life is the type of organisation that you are looking at.

An example: how much difference will there be between a job doing analytics at a Big 4 consulting firm in New York City, versus working in analytics in a large bank in Germany?

Why do we care? So that you know what you're getting into when you apply for a job. So you know the differences you might experience if you change industries, or if you take that international posting. So you can have a successful career.

Find your smile. Find the thing that you love and do that. If you are not insanely curious about the data that you are playing with, it might be time to find a different job. I can't cover off every possibility that could occur because that would involve knowing what is and isn't illegal in every jurisdiction around the world. All I can do is call out some of the things I have seen and some ways to handle those situations. Some of them are not specific to analytics, so you might want to explore alternate books to help you figure out how to respond.

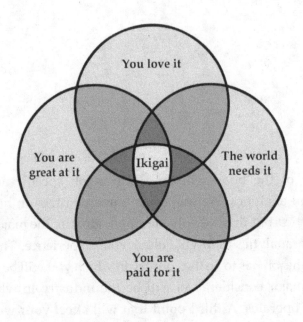

Figure 5 Ikigai Venn Diagram

Finding your smile is about getting to the centre of the Venn diagram above. It's about learning something and loving it and then researching where it fits in the world and how you can get paid for it.

Any career advice should be teaching you about these four circles. Think about recruiters – the good ones anyway. They take candidates (the top left two circles) and try to marry them the job openings they have on their books (the bottom right two circles).

Peter the Recruiter explained it to me thus: "My role is talking to hiring managers and taking their list of dry technical requirements and identifying what they really want. They don't usually really want a person with two years of PowerBI experience. What they're looking for is a data visualisation expert. They happen to use

PowerBI, but learning a new program isn't that hard. And would you rather have a person who has been developing dashboards for three or four years who may need six months to get up to speed with PowerBI, or a person with one or two years of PowerBI specifically as the total extent of their data visualisation experience? And on the candidate side, they usually need a hand exposing the business value that they've generated on their CV. They might have something like, 'Made dashboards for stakeholders,' and what they should be proud of are things like, 'Made dashboard that generated $1M of additional revenue.'"

For Peter, his sweet spot is going beyond the dry list of skills that the hiring manager presents him with. For him, the magic happens when he sees a person who is a great fit for a role but whose CV doesn't quite reflect it. And getting the candidate's CV to reflect how good they actually are for the job, and then convincing the hiring manager of the fact, is where Peter finds his smile.

Ikigai[9] is that sweet spot. It's where the employment market rewards you for generating business value while doing something that you are good at, that you enjoy doing. There are plenty of things that you love doing that you won't get remunerated for because you're not good enough. Playing the piano might be one of those things. You might not be good enough to play in an orchestra or play in a band. That doesn't mean that you shouldn't play the piano, just that you should maybe practise a bit more before deciding to do it for a living.

One thing to keep in mind in all the following discussions: all the advice below is predicated on a favourable economic environment. Raises and promotions are different propositions when the economy is in recession, or the business is making a loss. It's a good idea to keep that in mind when having discussions about pay, raises, bonuses and promotions.

---

[9] It's not actually: https://ikigaitribe.com/ikigai/ikigai-worksheet/ (but we can still use the concept even if we are mislabelling it).

CHAPTER 5

Cultural Differences

Any sort of guidance on your career will be driven by who your employer is, where you are working and the industry in which your employer operates. Some of those differences will be a result of the size of your employer – your experience and opportunities in a large multinational will necessarily be different than those you experience should you be working for the local dog grooming salon. Likewise, the culture of your work environment will be a combination of the market in which you work, plus the culture of the head office – and being aware of conflicts will allow you to navigate your career a little better than others. And of course, the nature of the business your employer carries out has a huge influence on the culture and your experience while working there. Let's have a look at how the differences in a business change the experience of working in the analytical part of the org.

Agency/Consultancy/In-House

Agency

Agencies are those firms who are paid to do something that could be done in-house but for whatever reason they do not want to have those resources in-house. No judgement. But because of this, you have a focus on satisfying the client requirements. Typically, the sort of work that you may be asked to do can have a data manipulation component. The agency exec loves the data type of work because of the great margin (set it up once and charge a regular subscription, and only have to spend additional money on it if something breaks). But the transactional nature of these arrangements means that they are at risk of being replaced by a lower cost provider. A successful exec in an agency explained to me that the best way of customer retention was to also do in-depth analytics for clients, and to exceed their expectations with the deliverables. The way they explained it was that even though there was less margin (paying for all those pesky analysts!), the opportunity to get embedded was well worth it. Success in this case consisted of presentations in which were 75% of content covered the client requests; "Ok: that answers the question I asked." 20% of the presentation content should then cause the client to perk up and say, "Oh: that's the implication of what I asked for." The remaining 5% should dedicated to making the client's jaw drop as the agency explains what they *should* be doing and the size of the opportunity. The goal here should be to produce analysis results that are something the client will be able to take to their boss and make them look really good.

Working for an Agency is a great way to learn pure analytics because the whole business is an analytics business. Success here is driven by customer satisfaction, but the challenge is getting the insight into the customer business without having to talk to them – the client/agency barrier can make it hard to deliver really good insights.

Agencies are frequently purchased and merged into businesses who can resell their services, but which are not necessary agencies themselves. This could be a marketing agency buying a digital agency to unlock their ability to generate web traffic insights for their client base. Or it could be a credit agency buying an analytics agency for their loan decisioning product or their superior Probability of Default algorithm. In those cases, the culture of the analytics org can very easily change; they are no longer pure play analytics orgs, but an analytics org in a marketing business in the first situation, and an analytics org in a financial services business in the second.

The point here is that the nature of the ownership of the business has a direct effect on the culture within the business and therefore your potential work environment.

Consultancy

Consultancies are interesting, regardless of the size. When I worked in Forensic Data Analysis at EY, I was in what was considered an IT function within a division run by lawyers within one of the big 4 accountancy firms. A few steps removed from the core of the business! Consider how those differences might manifest themselves in the culture of day-to-day life. IT is different from lawyers who are different again from accountants. And each level is ripe for the possibility of cultural conflict.

Consulting is run on the concept of utilisation: how much of your time the business can charge to the client. As you move up the hierarchy you have more and more responsibility to bring in more business yourself. But typically, it's like Agency work. The work that is done is directly billed to the client. So, the business itself is analytics.

In-House

In-House analytics is what I call it when there is no direct connection between the costs of the analytics function and the revenue generated by the business. This is where the implementation of the recommendations from analytics are carried out by the funding business function rather than from analytics. It's the most common situation for an analytics org, in my experience.

So why is this important? Where analytics sits is important because it changes the culture slightly, not only in how the business thinks of analytics but also how analytics thinks of itself. Consider: in an agency, analytics *is* the business. Funding, and therefore resourcing comes directly from revenue. So, if you are looking for promotion or leadership opportunities, there is a connection to the bottom line, which is quite transparent. In Consultancy, analytics is a product, sold by the hour. In an In-House scenario you are an expense. So, on one hand the business has an incentive to keep your team small because they are paying for it out of their budget, but on the other hand they have a list of things they want built and a list of questions that they want answered.

Language

It's been said many times that the UK and US are two countries separated by a single language. English is full of idioms that can be fertile ground for miscommunication – even for those where it is their native language! An example: an analytics manager had called a meeting with a number of her stakeholders, which she expected to get a little heated because of the subject matter. Her boss was in the room as well due to the expectant fireworks. The analytics manager was an American, and everyone else in the room was European. It started off well enough, with the manager cleverly leading the conversation around the big flashpoints, although as if under the influence of gravity, the conversation kept returning to a sensitive topic and threatened to get out of hand. The analytics manager could see this and so said, "Let's table that topic." The stakeholders leapt onto the topic and had a heated conversation. Both sets of stakeholders forcibly presented their opinions and, surprisingly, thrashed out their disagreements and came to a positive conclusion. As the participants filed out of the room, the analytics manager's boss pulled her aside and said, "I'm really impressed with how you handled that conflict in the room. You were very brave to bring that to a head."

The analytics manager, still feeling a little shaky in the knees, responded. "I was actually trying to take it off the agenda! 'Table that,' in US-speak means to put a pin in it, to postpone the discussion."

A very good senior manager in a multinational put it very succinctly: when you're dealing with cross-culture divides (and here they made a point that not all cultural differences cross international borders), you have to be more deliberate in your communication. In particular, when dealing with the US, be clear and upfront, they don't like nuance and you can't assume that they get your sense of humour. Give specific instructions and be very clear on the timeframes and deliverables.

Country

I could write another book just on what it's like working in different countries. The different laws and attitudes imbue each workplace with a full set of unspoken expectations and power balances between employer and employee, of which it is wise to be aware. The culture of a workplace is not just dictated by the country in which the job is located, but also of the culture of the country of the head office, and to a lesser degree by the culture of the country of the manager.

What this means is that you could have a job in the UK, managed by an Australian and working for a firm that has a head office in the US. So, you would have an employment contract governed by the

UK legal system, the US head office trying to set policies that may or may not be compatible with the local employment law and you might also have the manager putting their own spin on things.

If I had to categorise the differences between countries, the simplest starting point would be identifying where the balance of power is regarding employment protection. As in, how hard it is for an employee to be let go or fired. The OECD publishes comparative statistics[10] on how hard it is to fire employees in a number of countries, some of which may make for some surprising reading if you have been in that position.

It can be hard for those who have not worked in the US to fully comprehend just how few protections employees have other there. As one interviewee put it so succinctly:

> All the laws and regulations are entirely focused on the employer and there are little to no laws protecting the employee. Employees serve at the behest of their employers and can be let go at any time for any reason, or even without a reason. There is a vast cultural difference between working in the US and other countries.
>
> Many places don't have vacation and sick leave anymore, it's all referred to as PTO (Paid Time Off) and you have to take PTO any time you're away from the office even if it's for sickness or injury. There is far less PTO awarded here too... most people I talk to only get 2 weeks PTO each year, so you can imagine it only takes having the flu for a week and you're pretty much done!
>
> They're also a bit foreigner leery here, and I'm sure that I've been turned down for roles simply on the basis that

---

[10]https://www.compareyourcountry.org/employment-protection-legislation/en/0//ranking/

I'm not a small-town quarterback and I speak different.[sic]

I frequently see on social media references made to the number of holidays that employees in different countries are entitled to. According to Medium[11], Austria is the winner with 38 days (25 annual leave and 13 public holidays) while the US does not have a minimum legislated annual leave allowance.

But the biggest difference was summed up by one of my European interviewees who said the following:

Americans talk about work/life balance because they see these two things in opposition. Work is only part of life.

I'm telling you all these things not to make you want to move to Europe, but to let you know the sort of adjustments you might have to make should you move internationally. Or, if you take a secondment in a foreign office of your employer. And when you do go to a foreign country for your job, be very clear on which set of holidays you take. I don't know which is weirder, celebrating July 4th in the UK (celebrating the US independence from Britain while in Britain) or not turning up to work in the US because it's St Andrew's Day in Scotland.

You will notice that I have not sought to explain away the differences between people of different countries by referring to cliché or stereotypes. I'm not going around saying that Americans are this way or say certain sorts of things. The Irish are like this, or the Germans do that. I would recommend you also steer clear of this casual racism.

---

[11]https://medium.com/skeptikai/top-30-countries-for-paid-leave-holidays-8c9b7aaf9032

In the world of offshoring, there is yet another instance in which you should be aware of international differences. I have first-hand experience in managing offshore teams in India, Poland and Ukraine, and it is yet another layer of complexity to be managed. Again, there are a lot of books and resources out there to guide you through managing your offshore relationships.

Academia vs Industry

I have talked to only one person who had made the jump from academia into industry to pursue a career in analytics. The biggest advice that this person gave me to pass on to those following in their footsteps was to adjust their contributions.

"There's an attitude to authority within academia that anyone can challenge any idea and thrash it out in public with the concept that this will lead to the best ideas going forward, but in industry sometimes you're just getting a task to do and shouldn't try to thrash out the minutiae. It took me way too long to figure this out and I got a reputation for being argumentative until my boss pulled me to one side and had a little chat."

There's obviously a nuance to challenging your boss, especially in public. Learning where that line is may involve a couple of "calibration meetings."

"We talked about it and agreed to calibrate the appropriate level of challenge in our weekly chat. After a month it wasn't needed anymore because I had learned where that line was. But I still had a certain reputation with my stakeholders."

In general, the approach in academia to finding the best solution is not appreciated in industry. The most sophisticated approach is not necessarily the best approach: as long as the approach is simple, transparent and explainable it only needs to generate 80% of the benefit.

And more importantly, you have to care that the artefacts that you create are used. You cannot have an arm's length detachment from what you generate for work. There has to be a connection between your work and the business, otherwise you are not earning your pay check. Let me quote from one of my interviews:

"There may be a disconnect between the thing you created and your ego if you are in academia. Sure, you're proud of the work you did – you can point to the reasons you used this or that equation or formulae and the mathematical approach, but if your funding agency decides to go in a different direction, do you really care? In industry, the metric of business value, if not actually in dollars and cents, is in attention – how embedded your artefact is in the business process in which you support. If you are producing dashboard after dashboard and nobody looks or uses them, are you creating business value?"

Profit vs Non-Profit

Let's split non-profits into two: the first is the "passion project" for someone who is privileged and has the resources to spend the time on their pet project. In this situation they are plugged into wealthy people who they generate funding from and sometimes (in my experience) extract a salary that is out of proportion to the positive impact on the supported group. In the worst case this is a person getting a £100k salary when the actual beneficiaries of the charity might get £20-50k. I hasten to add that not all charities are like this: but there are certainly some like it.

In this kind of charity, the founder's personality is writ large because it is *their* charity. As a result, if you are looking for advancement or even resourcing to do the job that you're paid to do, everything depends on your relationship with the founder.

The alternative to this is the charity that somehow puts the beneficiary above the people in it. Examples of this are the NGOs (Non-Governmental Organisations) – UNESCO, FAO, that sort of thing. It may include smaller charities in which the focus is on the beneficiary. I'm not saying that these organisations don't have personalities and ego, but simply that the organisation is larger than the individuals within it. In these cases, there may be rule books – it's always beneficial to read those and find out the rules. Bear in mind that this may also make advancement problematic, as new roles by definition are not tied to a budgetary process that is driven by profit or loss.

I also have noted that people working in these charities tend to have longer tenures. I have concluded that people working in the charity field tend to get paid slightly less than in the private sector and therefore only work there if the charity in question is dear to their heart. I bring that up because that ability to focus on something bigger than the individual will by necessity mean the culture will be slightly different from other workplaces.

Start-up vs Large Corporate vs Small Company

Start-ups have the benefit of having very few restrictions on what you can do, which is a double-edged sword as there are usually few resources to do the work. So, you find yourself shooting from the hip and making things up as you go. This usually is accompanied by a smaller salary and larger stock options than other jobs, as there is more reward tied up in the ongoing success of the firm. In terms of career advancement, this can give you opportunities to do things that you wouldn't have the opportunity to do elsewhere. Data lake in the cloud? When you're the only one doing analytics it's most likely to come to you. You probably wouldn't get to design, implement and build something like that if you were one of twenty junior analysts in the bowels of a global bank.

In a start-up, career growth is a series of opportunities resulting from the challenge of growing something from scratch. Formal career growth is typically not even thought about. The business is focussed on the next step in their growth (proving product/market fit, getting to revenue, breaking even, scaling) rather than providing formal steps to help in your career.

A large corporation is one in which specialisation becomes increasingly likely. This is where you usually find split roles – so you might have a Data Engineer who only moves data around, and a BI analyst who only builds dashboards. These tend to have more layers of roles so there are clear stepping stones in terms of a career. If you're lucky, there are career ladders to demonstrate the kinds of behaviours that you need to prove in order to qualify for these other roles. Hopefully, there is also a well-publicised promotion process to facilitate that advancement. If there are no career ladders, the large corporation will more than likely have the HR support and appetite to allow you to push for having one.

There's no excuse for a lack of career growth structure. It is possible to be ignored or lost in shuffles, and for your voice to be lost in the crowd. So, there are different challenges to be overcome.

A small company can be frustrating as you have the worst parts of both of the previous two categories. There can be an element of you doing everything, as well as a resistance to growing you in your career. This is because personal career growth is a risk to the business. As there are typically few opportunities for advancement, if an employee becomes dissatisfied with internal opportunities or feels that their growth is being stunted in any way, then their only solution is to move on. This leaves the business short of resources to do the job. In my experience in these sizes of organisations, there is less of a feeling of responsibility to provide any sort of career progression. They also do not have as much HR resource to support change or career progression.

Consulting vs Industry

Consulting differs from Industry in particular when it comes to promotions. It is possible in Industry to get a promotion by applying for a manager role in a different firm when all you have done in the past are IC roles. It is far less likely in Consulting roles, because you need the sponsorship of your manager and their peers.

In particular when you are at senior manager level in Consulting, you need to start bringing in your own revenue. You are far less likely to get a senior manager role in Consulting unless you can demonstrate that you have brought in revenue in a previous role. Compare this with a similar level role in Industry: without the revenue component there is a slightly easier path to such a role. But only slightly easier!

Government vs Private

Similar to the Non-profit sector, when you are dealing with a Governmental role (whether that is local government such as a council, or central government for a governmental body), the language changes. While in a profit-driven environment you might have customers, products, stores and sales, in the Government sector you could have funding cycles, service providers, programs and outcome. Being able to talk that talk and understand how those elements relate to each other will help you understand the job better when working for a government employer.

Additionally, when there is no profit imperative, there are other outcomes that your employer is trying to maximise. This could be anything from delivering positive health outcomes to making sure nuclear waste is responsibly disposed of. Working for these employers means that it's imperative you understand the primary drivers of those firms and how the work that you do drives the business towards those goals. If you come from private, profit-fixated industry analytics teams, making that adjustment will probably be the biggest cultural shift that you need to make prior to being able to advance in your career.

CHAPTER 6

Breaking In

How Do I Get A Job In Analytics?

The easiest way of getting a job in analytics is to have a job in analytics. That's not helpful, is it? Especially if you are trying to cross-train and break into analytics from a different field, or you've just graduated with a fire in your belly but nothing on your CV. So here is some advice on how to get into analytics.

No Experience?

What if I am just starting out and have no experience?

You could volunteer for a charity and try to help them to use data and analytics to solve their pain points. Just be upfront with them about your experience level.

Or, if you really have no experience then you can literally manufacture it. There is plenty of data out in the world and I imagine that you have an interest that sits outside analytics. So, have a look at something that you are interested in and think about what you want to know. Emma Cosh liked the DiscWorld novels by Terry Pratchett, so she did a data visualisation[12] of which characters are in which books. Her viz is a lot more substantial than the screen shot shown, and is worth a look.

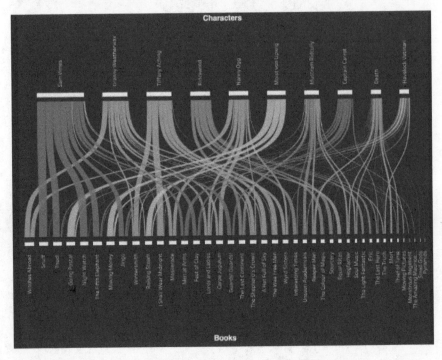

Figure 6 Partial Visualisation of DiscWorld Tableau Dashboard by EG Cosh (used with permission)

It's important to have a question in mind because you want to exhibit the business value equivalent. You want to show that you can understand a question, get the data to answer it and then present the data in a visualisation that answers the question. In Em's case the basic question was, "Which books should I buy if I like *this* character?" or, "Which books should I buy if I like *this* story line?" And the visualisations she has produced do exactly that. If a recruiter saw that Em didn't have any work experience (not the

---

[12]https://public.tableau.com/app/profile/egcosh/viz/TheDiscworldVisualised/TheDiscworldVisualised

---

case: she's got a lot!), seeing something like this would go a long way to proving that she could do the job.

No Data?

If you do a Google search for the kind of data that you're looking for, you might discover a cool dataset available online, but it's possible the dataset that you are looking for doesn't exist. If you aren't after something specific, you might look at Kaggle[13] or Google[14] datasets. More importantly though, it adds to your compelling story if you sourced the data using a tool you want to show a technical ability to use, to download the data from the web. Using Python to scrape a website for the data you need for a cool visualisation demonstrates proof of both the data visualisation tech as well as the capability to use Python (my lawyers insist that I warn you not to breach a website's terms and conditions in generating your datasets).

Too Many Interviews?

It can be difficult to maintain interest when you have answered the same questions time and time again. For my first stint at TripAdvisor, I had seven interviews and the second time around (after they'd changed their name to Tripadvisor), I had six. I recall my energy levels sagging noticeably midway through those first seven interviews, and I couldn't think of how to rally. I was saved by the interviewer asking me about my next trip. My enthusiasm for travel came through as I explained exactly where and when I'd

---

[13]https://www.kaggle.com/datasets
[14]https://datasetsearch.research.google.com/

be going next. That saved the interview because the interviewer could report back with complete honesty that I loved travel.

My advice? Try to find your spark and let each person see it. Have a range of questions to ask them – I made the mistake in one non-stop series of interviews (not for Tripadvisor) of saying to the fifth or sixth person, "No questions: they've been answered by everyone else." That robbed the interviewer of the opportunity to give their opinion on the employer, and gave them the impression that I wasn't interested, even though my response was borne out of interview fatigue.

My Questions?

One of the worst things you can do is not have any questions ready for the interviewer – and arguably worse than no questions are only selfish questions. The questions that you ask expose your thinking about the job, and the best ones are focussed on the success criteria for the role.

Please don't ask the following questions:

- How long do you get for breaks?
- How strict are you on drug testing?
- Can I get an advance on my first pay?

There are many books on this subject, but I'll list some questions you might want to consider. Some of them come with warnings.

- If I get the job, what would I deliver in the first six months to be considered a high performer?
- What does success in the first x months look like for this role?
- What did my predecessor do well? What could they have done better?

These are low risk questions that tell the interviewer you're interested in the concrete targets for the role. If there is prevarication in the answer it may demonstrate that they haven't considered what specific tasks you will be given. This is fine if the person you're talking to is the HR rep but if this is your manager then it is a warning signal that they have budget to increase the headcount but haven't thought about which of the tasks on the backlog will be assigned to you.

How many people were promoted in the last year and how much did their salary increase, on average?

This is a dangerous question because although it shows that you are interested in being a high performer, it also puts the acid on the org to prove that they do indeed promote from within. More importantly, it demonstrates that you care about the impact on the salary of those promotions. This is a great question because it sets the expectation that you are looking at actions that would lead to a promotion, that it is very important consideration in your career decisions, and that you won't simply accept a paper promotion – you're looking for something substantial in terms of a salary increase. What you're looking for is whether there is an HR rule that caps the increase of salary that comes with a promotion. It's a piece of knowledge to have because it demonstrates where there are arbitrary limitations on your career progression.

What is the reason this role is available? What is attrition like for this role/this department?

These are a little bit mean because you are implying that there is something wrong with the department. But it does give them the chance to explain that the role is as a result of expanding the team rather than replacing someone who couldn't handle unreasonable managers or stakeholders – or the toxic person in the team. If they can't give a view on attrition they might stop and reflect on how high or low it is, then and there.

Are there advancement opportunities if I decide that I don't want to manage people?

This is a good question because you're focussing on advancement and high performance, and you're also identifying where there might be manager level pay for a role that does not have management responsibilities. Rest assured that in any good company there will still be more responsibilities if the pay rises to that level, but the recognition that your contributions to the success of the company do not stop if you decide you don't want to manage people reflects well on the employer. A caveat here is that even with a framework that includes a manager-level IC role, there can be issues achieving the responsibilities to support the promotion case from both an institutional and personality basis. One org that I worked at had generic analytics targets that were totally inappropriate for the type of analytics that one analyst was doing. This meant that there was no way that they were going to be promoted.

How many hours did you work each week this past month? Are there regular crunch times when you need to put in extra effort?

This is a dangerous question because it shows that you care about your work life balance and that might be a challenge to your prospective employer. Their response will tell you all you need to know about the hours required to do the work, and the expectation of where the power balance is regarding anything more than a 9-5.

Bad Questions

The questions that you are asked in job interviews tell you a lot about the person asking them. One person asked me why they should hire me if I was just going to leave in a couple of years. What I would have liked to have answered with was, "Why do you think I will only last two years? How long would you like me to stay? And how long will you expect me to stay if the job is nothing like you have described, or there are personality conflicts, or cultural conflicts, or the opportunities you promise aren't there?" Instead, I gave them, "Oh, if the work is as interesting as you say, there won't be any reason for me to leave in a couple of years," but the sheer arrogance of the interviewer was on full display.

I had one hiring manager ask me:

"How many ping pong balls would fill a 747?" Of course, they will justify these questions by saying that they demonstrate how you think and that's the process they're testing. But you know what I think? I think these questions or brain teasers are power plays designed to show that the interviewer is the smartest person in the room. They're tedious.

One senior manager I spoke to put it quite succinctly. "When I'm hiring, I care about two things. Can they do the job? And can I get on with them? Unless the analytics job is ping pong ball or 747 related, I don't think that those questions would be needed."

It is tempting to let the hiring manager know that they have just asked a bad question, but in my experience that never ends well. The hiring manager has decided to ask that particular question, so they believe that it is appropriate. Calling attention to why it might not be will not make you any friends. But what you can do is add those bad questions together with all your other impressions about the hiring manager, so that they contribute to your decision about whether you decide to take the job (assuming that you receive an offer). If the questions make the hiring manager come across as a pompous ass, how satisfying will it be to work with them? What if they are strutting around the office like a peacock because they are the most intelligent person in the room? Never forget that you are also deciding whether to work with them, as much as may seem that they hold all the cards.

Nerves

Desperation is not sexy. Being confident in your abilities is sexy. Saying yes to everything is not sexy. Having solid examples of scenarios or situations in response to the obvious questions is sexy. Falling off your chair and spilling water all over the desk because the chair was on rollers and you didn't notice until you were halfway to the floor is not sexy. One way to get rid of the nerves is to practise (answering questions, not the falling off the chair). You can do so with friends (give them the list of questions but don't be afraid to ask them to go off piste), or just by yourself. It is more beneficial with another human being, though, as they can give you feedback on your body language, your tone of voice and how you handle the unexpected.

I've done a lot of interviewing, not only for this book, but also to hire people. And I know that it's possible to be too confident. I still recall one interview in which the candidate had obviously decided that they were going to say yes to everything. "Do you have experience with this tool? With this one? How much experience with this one? Tell me about a time you used this tool." My increasingly probing questions were answered vaguely and my questions about problematic scenarios were answered with situations that could have been from a job interview coaching website. Rather than coming away thinking that the candidate was a perfect fit for the job, I was convinced that I could not trust a word out of their mouth. So, your prepared answers have to be genuine. They have to feel true.

You can unlock interviewing success by practising the process of interviewing, but it's also important to unlock the confidence in your abilities by being aware of what your strengths and accomplishments are. You should update a brag sheet throughout the year that notes all the pieces you've delivered. Re-reading it before you go into an interview is a good way of giving yourself a boost. You can also always practise your anecdotes so that they come out a little more polished and eloquent.

Take Me With You

Have you ever noticed how in professional sports, when a new coach is hired, they usually bring their own assistant coaches from their previous job? You can imagine why; the head coach has worked with them before, they can trust them to do the job well and in the way that they want, and they enjoy having them around. They're not unknown.

In the same way, some managers have staff that they take with them into their new roles. Because they know that they will deliver, they know that they will operate in a way that reflects well on the manager, and the staff know that they will be looked after by the manager. It's impossible to give guidance on how to become someone who is asked to come along when the manager gets a new role, because you can only guess which manager that might be. But if you wanted to judge performance, ask yourself – who would I take with me if I was promoted into a new role in which the actual work is the same as what we're doing now? Who would I say yes to, if they got a new role and needed someone to do what I do now, in the new place? The more astute among you may be looking through your employment contracts (required in NZ, common in UK, rare in US) and noting there is a clause that specifically prevents the occurrence of this "poaching." My lawyers would also like to point out that I'm definitely not advocating circumventing clauses in your employment contract that prohibits poaching staff. But there are obvious ways of getting around those clauses, because it happens so often. One person I interviewed (and again, I'm not advocating these actions) said that these restrictions are impossible to enforce and that all it takes is a word to the new HR team to encourage them to reach out to this particular person on LinkedIn to see if they are interested in a new role.

Very early on in my career somebody was telling me about this phenomenon (clumps of workers who know and work well together, moving from firm to firm) and they looked at me condescendingly while asking me if that had ever happened to me. I, at that time, had only been in the workforce a little while, so thought the question unfair. "No," I admitted.

"Ask yourself why."

At the time, that was just mean. But now I can see what they were getting at. Think about your network of everyone you've ever worked with. Now think about how many of them you would reach out to pull into your team if you were a manager. And likewise, how many of them would reach out to you if they were a manager? Feeling that tap on the shoulder and having someone say, "Hey, I know you, I know your work, come work here for me," is incredibly rewarding. And being the person bringing the talent into your workplace is also rewarding (hopefully financially, via a referral bonus) because you are showing the strength of your social bonds. And being part of those social networks who give and get career opportunities is very valuable.

CVs

Many books and blog posts have been written about how to tailor your CV for particular jobs or industries, so I won't try to go into too much detail here. However, one of the awesome pieces of advice Peter the Recruiter gave me was to change my CV to demonstrate the business value that I was able to generate in each role I had. Originally (and we're going back a few years now!) I would have something like the following:

Making dashboards with Tableau, generating the data from a combination of sources including Hadoop accessed via Impala plus MS SQL and Alteryx.

I thought that was good as it was concise, and it hit all the technology product names I had heard were important to get through the keyword matching programme that the HR teams used. But from the business point of view, there was no indication as to whether I had been successful using those technologies. It performed much better when changed to something like this:

Reduced data disputes by 25% by proactively flagging data issues, saving 20 hours investigation work each month.

Then, at the bottom you can include a list of tech to satisfy the keyword matching. Keeping the business value front and centre in your CV allows the hiring manager to see that you are laser-focussed on generating business value, measuring it and reflecting upon that value in your list of career achievements.

PART 4

Guidance for Individual Contributors

At last! Advice for those who are in analytics! Well done for making it this far. Hopefully this part of the book will have the nuggets of insight that you are looking for. A word of warning, some of this may resonate with you and some of it might not match what you've experienced. I make no apology for that: what's presented is based on my experience and that of the people I've interviewed. It's been processed through each of our lenses and the meaning extracted is based on our understanding and value systems.

The general advice I elicited from the people I interviewed for this book was incredibly similar, and the warnings all the same. There is a type of person who just wants to do their job. They show a cynical disdain towards the things that you have to do to get ahead – and those people inevitably get left behind. They become the bitter workers who are stuck in entry level roles and can't see that they are the authors of their own work story. Occasionally they will shift sideways in an attempt to get ahead, not realising that the issue is not with their workplace, but firmly between their ears.

CHAPTER 7

Getting Good

It's quite likely that you came to analytics because of its technical nature. I myself came from a web-dev background and my (at the time) more than ten years' experience in databases was very attractive to analytics employers. One in particular had been looking for someone with Big Data experience but the market was very sparse at that point in time (they'd been looking for nine months) – so they expanded the role requirements a little, coming to the realisation that no candidate could have the full complement of skills. Suddenly, people with a strong knowledge of data entered the scope, even if they didn't know Linux and Hadoop. And that was me.

Perhaps you liked the idea of exploring datasets, like some kind of digital Indiana Jones looking to discover the magic answer to an obscure question. Or maybe you liked the combination of technical data wrangling and data visualisation in the same role. Or maybe you just liked whatever tool you were using at school and asked, how do I make a career out of using this? Either way, you probably got the job because you knew one or more of the tools that your employer used and were happy to get an entry level role in the industry.

So, your experience of being rewarded is likely directly linked to the tool that you use. If you're from a school or course that taught you how to use the tool, you were probably judged by how well you used that tool. When you compare yourself to others, it's probably in terms of how cool their data visualisation is.

I've got some bad news for you. While your ongoing abilities in producing the artefacts that you are tasked to produce is important, in general, there are a different set of skills that will see you be rewarded. And the speed with which you recognise this and focus on working on those skills will directly corelate to the speed at which you advance in your career.

Again, this is not a universal truth. I cannot guarantee that what I say here will exactly match your experience. But it is something that I have experienced time and time again over a fifteen-year career in analytics, and has been borne out in interviews with over fifty practitioners at all levels of analytics.

It could be presented as the business unit saying that they want a "Partner" who they want to know the business inside and out and have the capability to suggest areas of insight that they should be delivering, rather than needing the business to tell them what they want.

Story Telling

I once had a team member who was well regarded by the business and held up as being the epitome of all that was good in analytics. They would stand up in front of the business unit that they supported and explain to their stakeholders what they should do and why, what the results had been of historically similar situations and what they could expect if certain actions were undertaken. Such was the compelling nature of his delivery that everyone left the meeting talking about how good it had been and how they would definitely follow the analyst's recommendations. I was impressed and spoke to him afterwards about his approach.

"I use their language. I hit key points as I walk them through the story and I know the numbers that are needed to back up each story point. The action plan is easy and any one of the people in the room could have come up with the presentation if they had the numbers."

However, they didn't mention the structure. The structure of a good presentation is something that takes a while to figure out. Here's the conversation I had with a colleague of the "Good Analyst."

"We were asked to figure out which product was selling the most at this time. We looked at the data and had to cleanse some that had been corrupted from a process that had a bug in it. We then ordered the products sold in that time period by the volume sold, the total revenue of those sales and the gross profit of the sales. As you can see, we sold lots of frozen chickens, although we made more profit with the fresh chickens."

The issue here is that everything is from the point of view of analytics. What's important to analytics? The ask. The problems analytics overcame. The results that we decided were important.

The fantastic analyst I mentioned above? This is how they might have structured their presentation:

"We ran some ads featuring frozen chickens this time a year ago and we wanted to see if it was worth doing again this year. We looked at the impact on the whole category before and after the ad ran and we saw that all our stores had a spike in sales across the subcategory, which then dropped in the smaller stores that we're attributing to out-of-stocks. This led to an increase in sales of substitutable products like fresh chickens, which was good because they had a higher margin. I'd recommend that we increase the stock in the subcategory to avoid pissing off customers looking for those bargains, even if we forgo the benefit of selling the higher margin chickens. Our increase in Contribution from the frozen chickens was worth £240k while we would have expected to make £300k from the same stores with the additional volume in chickens as a result of the ads."

"Category." "Out-of-Stocks." "Contribution" (contribution to net profit). Talking about the actual business problem, making a recommendation and having the talking points to back them up. You have to be able to ask the questions to elicit the reason for an analytics ask. If your boss simply comes to you and asks which products sold in a particular period a year ago, you are not being given the opportunity to have those discussions with the stakeholder and you are not obtaining the clarity of the analytics ask. Your boss may think they are saving you the time of sitting in meetings with stakeholders, but they are not doing a good enough job of digging into the reasoning behind the ask.

I was impressed with how the meeting had gone, so I talked to the analyst's boss to see what their technical skills were like.

"Lousy. They can tell a story but some of the maths and approach that they use are barely defensible."

I blinked in surprise. Later on, I approached the analyst directly and asked them about their technical ability. They volunteered that the technical side of the job wasn't their forte, but that they loved the story telling element.

Now, I imagine that you may have a concern here. Are you telling me that I shouldn't care about correctness? About being exact?

A little. One of the questions I asked my interview participants was: "Who would you choose between someone who was technically able but needed to be taught to be curious and the business specifics, or someone who knew the business and its concerns but who required you to teach them analytics?" Time and time again they chose the latter. It's easier to learn the technical analytics skills than it is to learn the fundamentals of the individual business unit. This makes sense, because the business unit that you support will likely change from job to job. The analytics skills you need to apply get stronger and stronger the longer you stay in analytics, but every time you change roles you start from scratch in terms of knowing the business, and the concerns they have. These are the skills that will make your ascension meteoric.

Let's delve into the details of what you need to deliver to succeed in an IC role.

Business Knowledge

First, you must be seen as an expert in the area of the business that you support. In reality this means that you should have tools built that allow you to answer the questions that you are likely to receive. You should accept random questions about your part of the business and encourage others to ask the questions. And you must deliver the insights requested in a timely manner without impacting the other deliverables you're asked to do. This takes a little bit of preparation, but the benefits are immense.

Story time

It's been interesting watching how the data and analytics concepts have gained wider acceptance over the years. I worked with an analyst before there was widespread adoption of self-serve analytics. They went out of their way to get some OLAP cubes put in place on datasets that were incredibly valuable but hidden away in data centres (this was before the world put its data into the cloud). This allowed the data to be exposed to anyone with permissions and Excel, as the OLAP cubes used Excel very nicely as a front end. This by itself was not momentous, simply an example of some data being made available to a business that was not yet comfortable using it.

No, what made this a particularly good idea was that the analyst went ahead and built an extensive series of Excel spreadsheets on top of the data using the cubes. And they pre-filtered certain sheets to answer the questions that they always were asked. Did revenue increase or decrease week on week? Which countries contributed the most to the increase or decrease? What happened this time last year? Was the movement in revenue due to an increase or decrease in the traffic to the site, or to improvements or deterioration of the quality of the traffic? Were there particular campaigns that over- or under-performed?

Every morning they would come into the office (no WFH in those days), right click on the data sheet in their spreadsheet and select Refresh. If they had stopped there, they would have had a great tool for answering any questions that might have popped up from a swathe of stakeholders. Where this analyst really made their career is that they would spend the first hour of their Monday morning thinking about all the movements of all those parts of the business and they wore the hat of each of those parts of the business while thinking about the metrics that would make sense to them. They identified what they would care about.

So, the country account managers would be told that their revenue had dropped by x%, which was unusual for that time of the year as the previous year had seen an increase of y%. The primary drivers of the change were conversion, traffic or spend. The marketing teams would be told that the revenue from this or that campaign was skewing the revenue by $x. The SEO teams would be told that the increases in traffic that they had been working so hard to get were of low quality and converting poorly. Because of these highly targeted insights, delivered with very low effort on an almost automatic basis, and all the tools pre-built and ready to answer the next question and the next one and the next, this analyst was very quickly promoted.

Are you an expert? Do people come to you with questions about your area of expertise? What would you have to do in order to gain that reputation? What tools would you have to build?

OK, Have Tools, Now What?

Once you have the tools to quickly deliver insights, you must be curious. You must dig into the day-to-day activities of the stakeholders that you support. The goal here is to know what they do, what sources of data they use to generate which insights and the data points to decide what they should do next. You have to do this across the board for all the people in the team, so that you build up a picture of all the processes that your stakeholders follow. In theory this should make people think that you want to do their job. Why do you need to so much about their lives?

Two reasons: first, you need to build rapport with your stakeholders and one of the best ways to do this is to show interest in what they do on a day-to-day basis. Some of that is simply spending time with people, but in this case it goes deeper. You're not only looking at the goals and objectives of their business unit but how the individuals drive towards those goals. What they do and why they do it is really important. It also identifies where their business unit interfaces with other parts of the business and the sort of data that you are likely to be asked to use in the future.

The other reason is that if you have a list of the goals of each of the individuals and how they roll up into the business unit as a whole, you can start to think about the sort of things that would move the needle for them – before you are asked. You need to talk to your stakeholders about the type of things that may or may not work for them and the reasons why. This will demonstrate that you care and that you are thinking in the right terms, so that when your stakeholders talk among themselves they will be talking about you in terms of proactiveness.

The essential thing to learn from the business unit is the values that they apply to each of the parts of their roles. You are looking for the things that will move the needle the most. And when you suggest something and you get a shake of the head, it's important to know why what you have suggested is such a bad idea. It will give you more insights into the thought patterns of the stakeholders and inform your next idea, and your next.

"Are you saying that I don't need to know my technical tools? I don't need to know SQL and Tableau, for example?" Not at all. The HR team has key word recognition on all the CVs that come across their desks and if the hiring manager says that you need SQL and Tableau, there better be a bunch of mentions of both of these in your CV somewhere, otherwise the AI won't trigger on your CV and you will fail at the first hurdle. No, what I'm saying is that you need a certain level of your technical skills, but that your advancement in your career will not thereafter rely on those technical skills. They become a necessary element but not a sufficient element of your promotion case. This can be a hard message to hear, because at the beginning of your career the only reason that you have gotten the job is because of these technical skills, and you've probably worked hard to learn those skills, and so therefore it is disheartening to learn that you won't be promoted off the back of just having those skills.

How?

How do you get time with your stakeholders? How do you learn about the business? You might have to go outside your comfort zone here a little. There's a joke that you can tell the extroverted analyst because instead of looking at his shoes when you talk to them, they look at your shoes instead. But there is an element of truth there – most analysts I know aren't generally outgoing people. So, here's a little advice on how to get over that:

Most people I have encountered are very happy to talk about their job. And most are ok to spend a half hour talking to you about what they do. The best time to book this in is when you first start a job, but there is no reason that you can't reach out and ask any of your stakeholders for some time to have a chat. Use the words, "pain points" and, "your KPIs" to show that you are looking to come away from the meeting with a better understanding of what they need to hit their targets and make things easier for them.

If you are shy, feel free to script conversations. It can really help to make notes to help scaffold the conversation. If you're doing the meeting virtually you can have your notes on the topics you want to cover sitting on your screen right beside your video browser. The aim is to show genuine curiosity about this person and what they're trying to do and why. Don't be afraid to start at the macro level. Why are you doing *this* thing? What KPI does *this* relate to? How much does *this* have an impact on your bonus? Do we in analytics have any impact on how you do this yet? Where do we fit in?

And while they're talking, you should be taking notes on what they're doing and how. Resist the urge to come up with a lot of immediate things you can do to make their life easier. Don't be afraid to ask the stupid questions. Preface them with, "This might be a stupid question, but why are you using this tool instead of this tool?" The overall impression that you are aiming to demonstrate is that you are curious and open. I've never had these sorts of conversations without feeling that there was something that I could do or make that would make things easier for the person. It is vital that you don't make any promises to them at the time. If they eagerly ask, "So, can you do – " feel free to say things like, "Let me go away and look at my notes and have a think about things," or, "I can think of a couple of things but I need to talk to my boss about where that might fit in our priorities," or even, "I need to ask a few people about the technical part of a plan that's slowly formulating. I can't promise anything but let me talk to a few people first." Don't be afraid to ask them to quantify the benefit of anything they come up with. "How long do you spend doing this task each week?" "How many other people do this by hand in your department?" The last thing you want is for the person you've just spoken to, to run away and spread the good news that analytics is going to come in and fix everything. You're probably able to put new tasks on the backlog but you might not have the power to prioritise.

Now here's a point that I found surprising: people remember emotions much more than rational arguments. Therefore, your goal should be that everyone needs to feel good about you. I'll let that sink in for a second. Even if you are not able to deliver all the things that you had in mind while talking to your stakeholders, the fact that you were interested in finding out about their job and their goals means that people will remember that willingness to talk and learn. Please don't sell vapourware: don't give them the impression that they will get solutions if you can't guarantee that. You want to build trust by developing rapport rather than damaging it with disappointment.

Now, here's another controversial point.

When I was doing my interviews, one of the points of agreement among the senior managers was that the biggest indicator of someone who didn't quite get it was that they didn't understand the "why." They explained this as the analyst not knowing why they were doing a piece of work. When asked to elaborate, they said that the analyst didn't understand the task and therefore there was too strong a chance of preparing an incorrect or incomplete analysis.

Now, I've been in that position before. On both the manager as well as the analyst sides. Here's what's going on. The analyst knows that they need to be closer to the stakeholder so that they can ask questions and reach a deeper understanding of the requirements. The manager, who is usually the one in the meetings with the stakeholder, thinks that they understand the requirements and so will argue that the analyst does not need to talk directly to the stakeholder.

This could be for two additional reasons: the manager might not want to impose additional time drags on the stakeholder, especially if they are adamant that they know the requirements. Also, they might not feel comfortable having the analyst ask questions of the stakeholder. It might be that the analyst has a confrontational attitude or alternately the kind of questions that they might ask may expose a limited knowledge of the data and therefore put the trust built with the stakeholder at risk.

The analyst is told that they have to understand the requirements and so will push to be present in the discussions. This in turn challenges the manager and their management of the workflow. And so, the analyst risks their relationship with their manager if they push too hard, and risks exposing weakness in knowledge to the stakeholder if they do get to be in the room, and risks not knowing the full picture if they don't.

Analysts should find out why their manager doesn't want them in the room with the stakeholder. Gently probe – phrase it in such a way as to be a suggestion for development opportunities. "I'd really like to be in the room for that meeting, but it sounds like you don't think that would be a good idea. Are you worried that I'll say something embarrassing?"

On the other hand, if you are the manager it's a good idea to assure the analyst that you are not worried about them saying something embarrassing, especially if that is the reason! Phrasing it as something like, "I think we need to work on the stakeholder relationship and part of that is working on the sort of questions that are likely to come up in that sort of meeting." If it's purely a workload reason, it isn't incredibly satisfying to hear that you're not wanted in that meeting because you're expected to be working on a different task. Whatever you come up with, please don't use something as generic as, "It's not appropriate for you to be in that meeting." The two takeaways from this issue for the manager are that it's a good position to be in: the analyst wants to get to the heart of the issue. And they feel comfortable enough to challenge the situation.

CHAPTER 8

Structure

Where to now?

Some people aren't ambitious. They are quite happy to sit in the back office and do their thing for years on end. Or perhaps they are happy to have the pace of their career progression determined by their manager. They usually say things like, "Oh well, I'll get a promotion when they're ready to give me one. My work speaks for itself." If these people are technical they may very well find their niche and if they're lucky and there is the adequate recognition of the value of what they do, then they can do quite well for themselves.

Let's not undervalue these people. These are the strong performers who won't clog up their managers' diary with demands for objectives and targets. These are people who don't want to know how they're getting on with those targets via regular updates and check-ins. From a manager's point of view, these are people who keep their mouths shut and simply do their job. When you're hiring, you rarely see these people because they don't come on the market very often.

But this isn't a book for those people. Those people are happy with the status quo. They aren't interested in managing their career. They're not looking for insights into how analytics works from a cultural point of view, and they're not looking for advice on how to get better at their craft. It may be that they have never thought about managing their career. They do the job, they get paid, they go home. If you were that kind of person and you're reading this book and you have had your eyes opened, welcome to your new world.

I worked at a bank once and asked my boss what I had to do in order to get a promotion. I expected him to point to a document online that spelled out the responsibilities, goals and objectives that would set in stone what I had to do in order to achieve my career aspirations. I was a little perplexed when he just said, "Get on well with your manager." That seemed a little self-serving, so I asked around and it was reinforced by the discussions I had with others. When I dug further into it, the answer was a little more nuanced and had more context: in the roles at the bank, they didn't really go in for a set of responsibilities for each role because the environment shifted so quickly that what was essential two months ago was either done by someone else or not needed anymore. And so, the relationship with your boss was essential because only they knew what you were being asked to do and how you were performing against those tasks. When I found that out, I frowned and asked, "But what if you disagree with their opinion on how well you are performing?" The answer was, "That's why you need to get on well with them – not to influence how they feel about your performance, but to find out what they think about it and why, and how you can change that perception by improving your performance."

One person I worked with as an IC would wait until the month before the annual performance management cycle began and then would make a great production of being a go-getter with a flurry of activity. They never got the promotion they were aiming for because it was so obviously a one-month effort.

Please Sir, May I Have Some More?

If you've spent much time in the workforce one perverse fact may have come to your notice. Money is easier to come by when a firm hires a new person into a role than when they promote someone.

Have you seen this situation occur? A person decides that they want a promotion or a raise. They go to their manager and say, I want £x. The manager says, "Hey, let me see what I can do," and comes back and says, "I'm afraid not." Then the employee hands in their notice. And all of a sudden, the manager runs off to HR and comes back with the £ or something close to what was asked.

And anyone who observes that situation will be asking themselves, "Why couldn't they come up with that money when the person asked for it? Why do they wait until the person has to resign? Because by then they have gone out into the market and looked for a new job and agreed to change workplaces. So, they have mentally moved on from their current employer. And so even if the current employer makes a counter-offer, the employee has moved on mentally and it's game over. Why? Why?"

Let's look at this from the workplace's point of view. Most HR functions have a standardised promotion/performance management framework that addresses these issues once a year. This means that the business can focus on the business for the rest of the time.

And the business can't afford to acquiesce to every demand for raises. There are usually budgets that are agreed for the year and there may not be allocation for the required funds. I know that's hard to take when the business might be making billions of dollars and you're asking for an extra thousand or two.

And here is what is going on at the manager level: the manager thinks to themselves, "Is this person a flight risk?" If they don't think that they are, then they might just turn down the request out of hand. If they go to HR and tell them that the business is at risk of losing the staff member, then they may or may not be able to make the offer of additional money. Regardless of whether they can or can't give the staff member the requested raise, think of the precedent set by giving the person additional money just because they will leave otherwise.

You're setting things up so that everyone can go to their boss and say that they need more money, or they will leave. And that is effectively holding the business to ransom (we'll ignore the situation where the business might be under paying people). Because if they cave and the rest of the staff learn that they can get another £x by threatening to leave, then all of the sudden the business is looking at a massive increase in the salary and wages bill. No business wants to lose control over such a large component of their expenses. It's also why sometimes you will get a discretionary bonus rather than a raise – if it's a one off then the increase is not baked into the ongoing costs of the business.

Not only that, but you are making no promises that the staff member who threatens to leave without additional money can come back a year, a month or the following day and say, "Actually, I need more." Negotiating with blackmailers is tricky because they keep coming back for more.

And in addition to that, it's a bad faith move. When you got the job, you agreed to do that particular job for the amount of money you negotiated. There are a lot of reasons as to why a renegotiation is warranted: you find out that the job is a lot more responsibility than first discussed, or the scope of the role has changed over time, or the cost of living has risen and now the pay on offer is not competitive. But if none of those are the case, and it hasn't been very long since you began in the role, then you could argue that "just wanting more money" is not really fair.

Businesses also make an informed decision about what bands they pay in, and how they compare to the rest of the market. Some actually have a policy that they will aim to be in a certain zone compared to the rest of the market. Some say, "We want to be 90% of the average for any salary survey." Or they might say, "We want to attract the best talent available."

It can be a frustrating practice to find out what the salary band is for a particular role, but you'd be glad to know that people in analytics are usually pretty accurate in terms of that sort of discovery. Why is that important? Because each band has an upper and lower limit. And so even if there is a desire to pay you more there might be institutional reasons that they cannot.

What's the manager's perspective on this? Are managers powerless to address staff leaving because of the pay situation?

I'd argue that if it gets to the stage that the employee is threatening to leave unless they get more money, then the manager has not done enough work prior to the discussion. What I mean by that is that the manager should know about their staff's career aspirations. They should know whether their team member wants to go for a promotion this year or not. Whether there are opportunities that they are looking for. How satisfied they are with their salary, that sort of thing. That also allows you to have the conversation:

"What has changed since our last career conversation? You didn't mention this then."

It may sound like I am on the company side of the, "Give me more money or else I leave," conversation and depending on the circumstances, I usually am. When you sign up for a job you are usually buying into the rhythm of the company when it comes to performance reward. To have the conversation about more money outside that system strikes me as being pushy. And the ultimatum part of the conversation has never sat well with me. It's confrontational and doesn't present you in a good light.

Now, there are a whole lot of reasons why it might be perfectly acceptable. If you were promised raises or bonuses and they did not eventuate. I've been there – the senior management were always promising that there would be a bonus pool, but come the end of the year there would be nothing. That would make the, "Give me more money or else I leave," conversation incredibly defensible. If you started mid cycle and they decide that this precludes you from getting a raise or a bonus or both. Again, if the rules are not fair and they won't accommodate making the situation equitable, why should you stay?

The important thing is that in countries with little employee protection, it is incredibly easy to overplay your hand. You never want to make an overt threat. And you shouldn't need to. When you have your conversation, never say, "If you don't give me a bonus or a raise or a promotion then I will leave." Here's what you should say. "I feel very strongly that ____. I think that you should ____. What do you think the chances are of that happening?" There are plenty of books that will teach you how to have those conversations. None of them are specific to the analytics world, so I haven't covered them here.

Please do not ask for a raise alongside the reason that you need extra money for x, y or z. They are reasons that management will not care about, so not only are you divulging personal information unnecessarily, but you are not moving the needle in terms of getting what you want. I mean, take that to the extreme: would it be ok for me to ask for a raise just because I bought a second yacht? No. It is ok to ask for a raise if you can't afford to live off what you are being paid. But it would be a good idea to have a backup plan just in case the answer is no. In that case and that case only the comment, "I can't afford to work here," might be justified.

If you have come to the point where you are, in effect, giving your employer an ultimatum, you have to be ready for the conversation to not end in your favour. That is why you need to dial back the inflammatory language. To give yourself wriggle room. If your conversation goes something like this,

"Hey boss, you've been talking about a bonus scheme for the past six months and nothing has happened. Unless you're going to give me a £5k bonus in my next pay, I'm going to leave."

"I'm sorry to hear that: HR are holding us up. So… was that you resigning, or…?"

I mean don't get me wrong, it feels great when you say it – you feel powerful. You're telling the boss off. But nothing good comes of it – it's not professional and most importantly, you will not get the outcome you are after. Compare it to this:

"Hey boss, you've been talking about a bonus scheme for the past six months and I really don't feel like I am being appreciated for all the good work that I am doing. Do you have any indication of when a bonus scheme will come into play? What will the criteria be?"

Your wording has to be professional and can't burn bridges. You can find translations from plain English into corporatese, but here are some to get you started:

When You Mean

Fiona and Stacey are useless. Why do they get the best jobs?

Say This Instead

When I started here, I was told that there was a strong performance culture.

When You Mean

You haven't done any of the things that you said you'd do, and I am sick of it.

Say This Instead

I am disappointed in the progress the company has made.

When You Mean

All my bills have doubled, and my salary has stayed the same.

Say This Instead

The salary increases we've enjoyed, while appreciated, have not kept pace with inflation.

So, how do you get what you want? Mostly by being awesome at your job. And then giving enough clues so that your manager knows that you are upset about how your performance is being remunerated and what would be an acceptable amount to keep you.

I can't stress how important it is to be widely recognised as a high performer before you have these conversations. It's not enough for you to think that you are good at your job. You want to be in the position that if your stakeholders and co-workers hear that you're leaving, they immediately tell your boss that they can't let you go.

The worst conversations are those in which you think you're brilliant, you tell your boss that you need x to stay, they tell you that's not going to happen and you walk slowly towards the door, waiting for someone to scream, "Noooo, you can't let them go!" And nobody does!

Career Ladders

That's why I like career ladders – they spell out the kind of things that are required at each level and take some of the subjectivity out of the situation. They can also allow you to reach agreement on judging whether you are performing at a particular level. What I mean by this is if you think that you are achieving all that is required from you and your manager disagrees, pointing to the outcomes required and identifying which ones you're not doing well enough is vital to addressing that performance gap.

I've worked at places that had a career ladder. One of them was defined so generically that there were digital analysts working on web analytics who were not covered by the responsibilities in the ladder. That would not have been such a terrible situation except their manager was too busy for regular check ins. So, they operated for a year with an expectation on goals and targets and at the end of the year they were told that what they had done did not meet the requirements. So, a career ladder in and of itself is not enough, but it certainly focusses the conversation and allows a more universal approach to goals.

I've also worked at a place where there wasn't a career ladder, but someone went out of their way to get one. Their job was made easier by the fact that there were actually three career ladders already floating around as historically, managers had agreed that there was a need for them, it's just that they had created them from scratch three different times. It was a good thing though, because it showed there was an appetite to have them, and someone had done a lot of the work to pull them together. It was therefore a simpler task of collating the three and validating that the resulting responsibilities were valid before getting HR to sign off on them.

If you are at a place that does not have a career ladder, how would you best put one together? The first step is establishing what level of support there would be for one amongst senior leadership. You would be wasting your time if senior management doesn't want them.

If they don't have one, how do you get one? It is possible that the org is too small to warrant such an investment. Because it will take the HR function a significant level of effort to put something together or to validate one that you provide. It is important that the ladder documentation is sufficiently specific to be measurable but also generic enough to cover all the types of analytics that are supported by the ladder.

I've worked in a few organisations who have provided concrete career ladders that outline the behaviours required to achieve any particular role. If the organisation has gone to the trouble to come up with these ladders, they usually have gone through the process of validating these with HR and in both of these orgs they have also recognised that there is an IC role that is paid as much as the manager role and has high focussed responsibilities but no people management responsibilities.

If your organisation does not have such a ladder or have the ladder but do not have a manager-level IC role, there are some conversations that should be happening with HR. Do not expect these conversations to happen quickly. But it is a good idea to kick them off and the key arguments for their existence is to reduce attrition and to prove maturity of the org. One of the best arguments for the career ladder is that high-end IC role. Sometimes it's called a lead analyst or principal analyst. The way to introduce the topic is to sit down with senior management and tell them that you are worried that the IC level staff do not have visibility on their career opportunities after the senior analyst role if they decide that they do not want to manage staff. Making a formal process or ladder with defined roles allows all staff to visualise a path on which they can stay with the company for a long time and be rewarded for the growing business value that they can deliver.

There are many reasons that the career ladder is not well defined or possible. It could be the case that a business is too small to need the ladder. An informal understanding might exist where when your manager moves on, the next most tenured staff member takes their role. The problem with understandings is that there are no guarantees, and it becomes difficult to plan your career if you do not know when opportunities will become available.

Don't get me wrong, even with proof that you are achieving the responsibilities outlined in a career ladder, if there is not the budget or existence of your target role, then you could find yourself disappointed at the end of the promotion cycle. Or there could be disagreement around whether you are meeting those responsibilities outlined in the career ladder.

Relationship With Your Manager

But that is the whole point of your relationship with your manager: to meet regularly and to consistently establish whether you are performing at a high enough level to warrant promotion. Additionally, it exists to establish the improvement areas you need to work on and whether the trajectory of your behaviour is sufficient for the expectation of a promotion in this round.

Your boss could be right. You might not be achieving the goals on the career ladder. Even in a less formal environment, you might not be achieving the goals that your boss has in mind for you. This is hard to accept, but the mature person's reaction to this is to dig into the details and find out exactly where you differ with your boss, and what you can do about it.

If you do not have regular check-ins with your manager, it is your responsibility to obtain them. That's a hard message to receive, but I will explain it. It is your career, not your employer's – and not your manager's. It is up to you to identify your career goals, find out what is required to meet those goals, and seek the coaching and guidance that you require to achieve those goals.

But surely it is my manager's responsibility to provide those? Nope.

Think about what happens at the end of the year if you have no career goals or have had no discussions with your manager about your performance towards goals. What happens? Do you automatically get the promotion? No, of course not – no senior manager is going to stand up and defend a promotion for someone where there is no evidence that they had performed to a high level. Or perhaps there is evidence, but nobody cares about those particular achievements. There would be all sorts of accusations of favouritism. So, if you won't be getting a promotion by default, you have to work for it. If your manager blows off your check-in or won't give you the feedback that you need, you have to be firm. You have to be persistent.

The first step is to figure out what you want from that year in terms of your career. There's nothing wrong with aiming for a good level of performance, rather than aiming for a promotion. But if you decide that you do want to go for promotion, you need to prepare and you will definitely need those regular check ins with your boss.

Then, you have to determine who is going to be in the room when discussions on promotions are held. You need to decide how you are going to go about making your successes visible to all those people throughout the year, so that they will chime in during promotion meetings.

Some of the things you should be listening out for in conversations with your manager include any reference to "time in role." This is a nuance that is easy to get wrong.

"You haven't put in your time," means something totally different to, "You're not there yet."

The first implies that there is a set length of time that you must be in each role before progressing to the next. The second response indicates that there are a set of behaviours or abilities that the manager knows should be met in that role, and your performance is not matching those expectations. It is vital that you tease out the details of those expectations and that you put a concrete plan in place to achieve those abilities or behaviours, and how you will demonstrate them.

If you have a suspicion that any reservations from your manager are purely around time served in the role, then make them spell it out. Try to draw out the behaviours from the time served because the manager could just be getting confused in their head about the actual requirement of being in a role for, say, two years, and the average person in the role taking two years to demonstrate the necessary skills before progressing.

Even if you agree with your manager that your performance is at a high enough level to warrant the promotion, there is more involved than that. What? Didn't you just say that the career ladder does a great job of tying an objective view of performance to achievement for the year? Two things: first, it's nearly impossible to achieve objective views on anything, let alone performance. Secondly, there is more involved than simply having your manager's support: there is usually some form of calibration, especially in larger organisations.

Calibration is when an organisation takes all the opinions on the performance of all the staff in that department and tries to make sure there is no bias. Career ladders do a lot of the heavy lifting here, identifying the levels of performance required. But there can still be disagreement among your manager and their peers as to whether the performance actually warrants the grade. An example of this could be seen in someone you've pissed off during the year.

One approach to this is to create what some people call a personal boardroom, but which I term the Rah-Rah Circuit. This is the list of people who you need to be in front of during the year. These are the people who need to know about your achievements.

One manager I spoke to mentioned that she achieved her promotion by talking to all the senior management throughout the year about the fact that she wanted to be promoted, and asking them what they thought she should be doing. This was a great idea because it got all those people used to the idea that she was looking for a promotion, it helped her identify early on where people might have an objection to her promotion and what she might have to work on and evidence during the year. This differs subtly from the Rah-Rah Circuit I mentioned earlier, in that the conversations the manager was having were specifically about the promotion. The Rah-Rah Circuit could include people from higher up the hierarchy or different parts of the business – and more importantly, may include the work that your team is doing if you have direct reports.

Everything is sales

A different manager sent out a weekly email to the whole business identifying all the things that they had done that week. They made the email funny and mentioned their volunteering, and as time went on and they received various promotions the number of achievements they mentioned grew to include their whole team's successes. I mentioned that there must have been reluctance or a cultural resistance to doing that, and they agreed, but they said that their mentors were all pushing him to go for it and he had to feel the fear and do it anyway (referencing the book of the same name). He also knew that he couldn't please all the people, and he kept the tone light, with a joke at the end. And he was always honest. There's a fine line there: it's important to be honest – but equally important not to throw other teams under the bus!

It's a challenging idea that your performance is not the only thing which matters in regards to your career advancement. And you can react in a number of different ways.

Zach Wilson[15] said,

> *Being annoyed with perception management was one of the big driving forces for why I left my corporate job. As you climb the ladder, it's less important that you do a good job and much more important that other people think you're doing a good job. This requires you to have many meetings and discussions about the good jobbing that you're doing and if you don't do these meetings well, it's quite a myth that your good work will "speak for itself." Unfortunately, there isn't an objective measure of impact and you're mostly at the whims of your manager and peers and if you don't have a manager who likes you, good luck ever getting promoted!*

> *Being a creator is different because the perception management is so broad that they'll find the tribe of people who like you. You aren't stuck with the 10-20 people on your team with one person having an extreme amount of authority over your compensation!*

> *Quit managing perceptions and start managing your life!*

---

[15]https://twitter.com/EcZachly

Zach calls out a very important point. He rejects it, but it's worth focusing on. Good work in and of itself will not get you promoted. (Usually). The level of management who are asked to make recommendations usually have too many staff reporting to them either directly or indirectly, and therefore just cannot have first-hand knowledge of the work that you have been doing and the impact that it has on your stakeholders. I'll pause there to let that sink in, and for you to think about what that means in terms of your activities and behaviours at work.

CHAPTER 9

Promotions

So, if you decide to go for a promotion, what do you have to do?

It shouldn't be a surprise to your boss. You should have a frank conversation to identify the sort of things that you would have to evidence for them to support your promotion. When you have that conversation it's important to listen very carefully to the responses. That can be hard to do when you are concentrating on the difficult conversation and asking for something that you believe that you are entitled to. Believe it or not, you are listening out for any incredulity in the voice of the manager. If your manager does not take what you're saying seriously, then everything else will be a waste of time. So, listening carefully is one way of making sure you are not wasting your efforts.

You are specifically looking for any weaselling words in the response. Anything like, "We'll see," or, "I'm not sure if that's a good idea." You want to zoom in on the reasoning behind the lack of support if there is no support given. There may well be good reasons but determining what they are can be difficult to extract from your manager and might well be hard to take from a personal view. If you are not doing good enough work to warrant a promotion, it's important to know – but it might be quite confronting to receive that level of feedback.

When I first started work, I was convinced that if I worked hard and delivered what was asked of me then I would be rewarded with raises, bonuses and promotions. My brilliance would be recognised and my ascension to the CEO role would be swift and unfettered. Let's just say I was blessed with an abundance of self-belief, a deep and pervasive blind spot regarding my shortcomings, and a naive understanding of the corporate world. If I had the opportunity to go back in time to give myself some advice, I wouldn't because I wouldn't have listened to it. But if I had ropes to tie myself down and an ice pick to batter the message home, I would have told myself the following:

Ah, you want to be promoted? OK, you need three things: you need to perform. Now I know that *you* think you are performing but your opinion doesn't count. Your boss needs to think that you are performing. I know that he doesn't see everything you do, so you're going to have to solve that problem. If you can't recognise the things that are causing your boss to say that you're not crushing it, then you are going to have to learn to put your ego to one side.

Because it's not enough for your boss to think that you're doing a great job. The next part of getting that promotion is to impress your boss so much that they would be willing to put their reputation on the line and recommend you for a promotion in a room full of their bosses and peers. These meetings are called calibration meetings. It's where the arguments about who should be promoted are thrashed out. And in a lot of cases, it's the most persuasive manager who persuades the rest of their peers and their boss that one of their team should be promoted.

This brings me to the last part of getting promoted. It's one thing to impress your boss so that they are an advocate for you in those meetings. What you need is for your manager's peers and boss to also be advocating for your promotion. You must be so good at your job that all the managers know it, so when your boss says in the calibration meeting, "I'm recommending that we promote C G Lambert," everyone in the room nods sagely and strokes their chin and says, "That makes sense."

Think of this as your promotion plan – it has two streams, one on the technical side and the other on the social side.

Stream One

You need to find out what is required to get promoted. You must make sure that you are achieving this. You must find out from your boss where your gaps are (technical skills, behaviours, relationships) and really work on them. This can be difficult because you must be able to receive the feedback from your manager, appreciate it and what it means in terms of your personal behaviours, and most importantly what you need to change going forward. Whether that's adjusting your attitude, learning how to do data visualisations better, or developing your skills manipulating data, you have to do the work to improve.

Stream Two

You need to find out who will be in that room for the calibration meetings. Assume to start off that it will be your boss's peers and their boss. Then, make a plan whereby your achievements will be known by these people. Add to this a plan to get them on your side because you are delivering business value for them. How do you do this? Or more importantly, how do you do this without it coming off weirdly? I mentioned earlier about a manager who asked their boss's peers what she should do in order to be promoted. That was her way of approaching this topic without making it weird.

Back when I first started working, I didn't have these two streams locked down. I didn't even agree with my manager's appraisal of my performance. This was because I lacked maturity and didn't realise that my opinion doesn't really matter. This is probably the biggest area you will need to work on as an IC in analytics. You need to be able to take feedback and come to terms when it differs from your version of reality. If you can't see your performance objectively, you at least have to be able to determine how to grow in the areas that have been identified for you so that you are making progress towards those goals.

Opportunity is Rare. Be Prepared

What I am about to tell you is consistent across all the levels we talk about in this book. And it is one of those takeaways that is universal across industry roles and functions. The time to perform is not just at the end of the year. It's throughout the year. You must be consistently performing. You will not know when the opportunity for a promotion will come up. And if you only pull out the stops at the end of the year, even if there is an opportunity, you won't be considered for it. Of course, if there is no opportunity then you definitely won't be getting it, but opportunities are not tied to the end of a performance year.

They come up randomly as a result of a merger, an acquisition, a new product, or something happening in the industry. They happen for a million reasons, and you want to be the first name that is talked about when they do come up. It will be because you do such good work, and people know what you do. If you think that you will be recognised by just doing good work, then I'm afraid that you're wrong. Just plain wrong. Being good at your job is necessary but it's not sufficient – and that doesn't change over time. If you're thinking that you can simply be a propellerhead and sit in the back room cranking out great dashboards and somehow that will lead to success, then if you only take one lesson away from reading this book, it's that you're wrong. Simply putting in your time will not lead to your success. The times when people were promoted purely on the basis of tenure are gone (in my experience). And surely you would not want to work for an employer who is so rigid as to just look at length of service in a role before giving a promotion?

Too Valuable to Promote?

I hear about people being told that they are too valuable to promote, and it always rubs me up the wrong way. You see, in theory you should be having a lot of conversations with your manager during the year. Very early in the year you should be talking about objectives for the year, and you should definitely be bringing up the fact that, "This year I want to be promoted," when you are, in fact, ready to be promoted. That conversation should then be followed by, "Tell me what I have to do to be promoted." And then very regularly during the year, "How am I doing against those actions we talked about to get promotion?"

So, if you hear the "Too valuable to promote," comment when you initially bring up the possibility of being promoted at the end of the year, it is obvious that you have to say something along the lines of, "I am responsible for my career, and I was hoping that this job would allow me to develop in the areas that I wanted to develop in. It looks like that might not be the case and I have an obligation to myself to maximise my opportunities. Are you saying that I won't have any promotional opportunities here?"

It may sound confrontational – and it is a little bit, but it is a professional way of determining whether what you want is consistent with what the employer wants. It should also reveal whether any vague promises of developmental opportunities are a lie. The point is that you will know whether you are wasting your time and energy, or not.

The worst case would be if you sat down with your boss and agreed on a course of action that would lead you to be promoted and you make great progress against that plan and have documented evidence of hitting each of the goals during the year. And then at the end of the year they say that you are too valuable. You never have an entitlement to a promotion, even if the business leads you on in this manner, but you are justified in your feelings of betrayal should these events occur. And if you have spoken widely about your desire to be promoted, and have communicated those expectations, then the poor behaviour of your manager should become more widely known.

Problematic Circumstances?

So, what if something happens that stops you from doing the above? What if your manager gets let go before the end of year promotion rounds and the new manager doesn't know you, doesn't know what you discussed with your manager and has differing opinions on the sorts of things that will lead to a promotion?

Or what if your manager constantly cancels or postpones your regular check-ins and you never get the coaching or guidance that you need to hit those goals that you agreed at the beginning of the year?

Yeah. That's hard.

You see, one thing is constant. The perfect workplace does not exist. The perfect manager does not exist. The perfect work experience does not exist. And I admit that the things I talk about as they should happen are sometimes a long, long way away from what you will actually experience. You might find yourself in the position where what you have been promised is not what you've received. Or what you think should happen is not matched in reality. And you will have to make a choice about whether it is worth staying. That's a choice only you can make based on the circumstances and the value you place on the various things you are told by your manager and others.

One thing you should never feel bad about is leaving a job. How you describe your reasons, if you do tell people your reasons, is something that you should be very careful about. The goal here is to be professional. Take all the emotion out of the words that you use. Focus on the economic transaction of your labour for the remuneration and other benefits that are on offer.

What can really derail your promotion case is if your manager leaves before that calibration meeting. If you haven't got your boss's peers on side, and your new manager has no idea what you've been doing through the year, you have no chance at all. This is especially true at consulting firms where there is a more adversarial approach to promotions (The Hunger Games, anyone?). If this does occur, you will have to rapidly look around and establish who can you align yourself with. You need a sponsor, otherwise you fall through the cracks.

Promotion = Success?

I fluctuate on this topic. Is promotion the only measure of success? Quite frequently HR teams will promote the idea of a sideways move as being somehow just as good as a promotion. I can see their point of view – if they can't provide progression, what else is available to mollify the ambitious worker? A change will allow the worker to be challenged as they come to terms with the new role –

there is new data to explore, new stakeholders to develop relationships with, surely that will satisfy the worker? I think that this works if the new part of the business is exciting in any way for the employee. Or if the employee was looking for a new challenge rather than the kudos of being promoted or the additional responsibility of being a manager. But frequently those are exactly the reasons they are looking for a promotion. So, while it benefits the employer to retain you as an employee, I'm not sure that you're necessarily getting what you want. But think of it this way: if the choices are up or out, and up is not on the cards in the immediate future and you don't really want to move on from the company, wouldn't it be better to stay with the firm until the opportunity does arise and still allow you to learn something new in the meantime?

PART 5

Guidance for Managers

Very few people enter a manager role in analytics without having been a practitioner at some point. We'll find that it's possible to be a senior manager without having been an analyst, but the nature of the manager role is that you must be able to coach, teach and assess the work that your team is doing, and so therefore you need to be able to do the doing. Because of that restriction, most people that find themselves in the role of manager have come from the role of IC and because of the reasons outlined in the previous chapter, they have fought hard to reach this role. Sometimes they've even had to change employers to get the opportunity to become a manager. And so, most of the time the answer to why you became an analytics manager is because of career progression. It's the next step in your career, the way to be recognised for your abilities and the work that you have done, and a way for you to get more remuneration in exchange for additional responsibilities.

CHAPTER 10

Getting Good

How to Excel

I asked a lot of my interviewees what made a good manager. One of them (let's call them Dan) started by saying, "Choose your employer and manage them well," which I thought was an interesting statement. I dug into that a little more deeply and what it boiled down to was a recognition of the importance of the relationship you have with your boss and your personal responsibility for taking on that relationship. So, it's not: deliver dashboards daily. It's not: get your team to deliver dashboards daily. To be a good manager you must zoom in on the relationship you have with your boss. Set up regular check-ins with them. Being of one mind when it comes to your goals and how well you are progressing on achieving those goals is important. It's arguably more important than what your team achieves because without the team helping you achieve the things that your boss wants, they're wasting their time and talents on things that aren't needed.

Your team is vital to your success, of course. Dan continued their thoughts on the matter by talking about how your team contributes to your success as a manager.

"You have to learn to delegate and trust. You have to empower others. And you have to give good feedback. Read that book on Radical Candour[16]. Coaching is hard."

All very standard responses and with plenty of books and courses to develop these ideas. But some of Dan's parting thoughts were the ones I enjoyed the most.

"Perception is reality: right and wrong doesn't matter."

What Dan meant by this was that senior stakeholders don't want an argument involving their perception of how things are going, and they don't want to be contradicted. Which for people brought up logically and who rely on data can be a little confusing. By shifting the context of your conversations with senior stakeholders to match their worldview you can get onside with those stakeholders easier. I must have looked confused when Dan first told me that, because he elaborated with an example.

"If a stakeholder comes to you and says that there are issues with your data, you win no prizes if you tell them that they are wrong. You're better off finding out *why* they think that there is a problem, investigate the situation and then come back to them with a solution to fix the data. If there really is no problem with the data, then it becomes a challenge to your diplomatic skills to address the issue."

Workflow Management

Part of your job as a manager is to manage the team's workflow. There might be a workflow process tool, JIRA or similar. And so, it may involve a lot of low value admin work. But the value you add

---

[16]https://www.amazon.com/dp/1250235375/

is not necessarily checking that every task has the correct status in JIRA, the real value is talking to stakeholders about the tasks that they want to see done, and why. Knowing and communicating the "why" a task is needed is one of the facets that differentiates the role of the manager from that of IC. Not only are you responsible for making sure all the work goes through the workflow management system, but you are also responsible for what I call "sideways tasks." These are those tasks that find their way into consideration without going through the normal process and are categorised (at least by those that come to you with them) as top priority and emergencies. While it would be easy enough to blatantly turn down any of these requests, it could be detrimental to your career to do so, which makes considering what to do and how to communicate that decision a political one.

Storytime

A newly minted analytics manager came to me with a tale of woe. They would have a rush of demands on their team's time every month without fail. Three different senior managers would come to them with a demand for analytics support. All at the same time. All, "Drop everything, the CEO wants to know the answer to this question," sort of thing. It was exhausting.

The manager wanted to know what they should do – these were people who could make or break a promotion case, as they all dealt with the CEO directly. I asked if the manager knew why these questions needed answers. They looked at me strangely and said very slowly and clearly, "Because the CEO wants to know."

I smiled. "Yes, I get that, but why are the requests all coming at the same time? Are the requests the same?"

No, they dealt with a similar range of products over the same time period, but were all from a different point of view. The logistics senior manager wanted to know delivery efficiency, the commercial manager wanted to know about how demand related to their pricing and the wastage officer needed to know what the disposal rates were.

All at the same time?

"They all turned up at my desk on the same day with a request that I get back to them by the end of the week. Each one of those analyses would occupy my team for half the week and all the other work would have to be put on the back burner. To meet their end of week deadline I would have to push the team to get a week and a half's worth of work out in a week. And in addition, I would have to go to the other stakeholders and tell them their projects would be pushed back. And this was happening every month."

"It sounds like the CEO is raising a question for these three execs and they are all coming to you with their own spin on whatever that question is for the CEO. So, there are two things you can do here. The first is to ask the three execs what the CEO is *actually* asking of them. *Specifically*.

If I had to guess I would say that in the case you presented to me there was an issue with availability of those products in that date range and each one of them have their own angle on it. They each want to tell their side of the story. That would confirm the reason they want to take your team's time. And you obviously don't want to piss them off, so you don't want to tell them no, but they must appreciate the impact these tasks have on the business. And if they keep being asked these questions by the CEO and they therefore require the ability to answer those questions at the drop of the hat, then you are going to need additional resources to make sure that you can achieve the goals.

Another question to ask would be why they need the analyses within a week. You might be able to do a side-of-desk investigation and get all three out the door across three weeks. But you really need to dig into why you are bearing such a large disruption. You might need a special team that handles CEO-level emergencies. I have worked at places that had such a CEO level team put in place, as well as those where the request for a special team was turned down. The unsuccessful place was tighter on resources, and we were never able to communicate how the CEO level requests were impacting the other work that we were doing as the CEO didn't really care, because that was operational and they weren't making the demands on the team's time. The stakeholders who were having their deliverables disrupted were not as important as the senior managers, so just had to wear the delays. The only positive part of that outcome was that the stakeholders knew that we were not the bad guys and knew that we were just as pissed off at the whole situation as they were."

Being a successful manager means finding a way to manage all the demands on your team's time – without annoying the powers that be!

Management Training

I asked the people I interviewed to score the level of support they got as brand-new managers. The scores were typically around 3/10.

A common story I was told about new managers was that they emerge, bleary eyed from the first three months of the job, barely coping. They know the technical side of the job, so they focus on that. They become an uber-IC rather than a manager. When and if they finally discover that they have to delegate and start farming the work out to the team, they spend all their time fighting fires and reacting to emergencies. After six months they are seriously reconsidering their new job and may even be looking for the door. What gives?

It's easy as an IC to sit in the back room and do the work that you need to do. In fact, to achieve flow[17] you must be uninterrupted. You need the time away from other people to concentrate on the work that you are doing. Flipping between two projects disrupts that flow. So, having time away from people is synonymous with getting work done as an IC.

When you become a manager, you know that the team has work that needs doing and you want to achieve it by contributing to the work, and the best way you know how to do that is to buckle down, isolate yourself and do the work. And if you are a better new manager, you will not try to do all the work yourself, but delegate to the team.

When you do this IC work as a manager, you run the risk of ignoring the other parts of the job. Fighting fires and emergencies, hunting down bugs, going upstream to discover where errant data is coming from, all these require you to be available to address the initial issue and then, there is the most important aspect.

To think about addressing the core cause of these issues, you need the time to think carefully and come up with a strategic plan to solve the problem. To do the tasks that differentiate the role of manager from that of IC, you need the time to think about which stakeholders you need to talk to, and which of their different tasks generate the best business value. In short, the tasks that the manager does that the IC does not do, all require the ability to sit and think. And perhaps talk to the stakeholders. But most importantly, they require the time and ability to think strategically.

---

[17]https://www.codecademy.com/resources/blog/how-to-find-flow-state-focus/

None of this is achieved by doing IC work as well. As Dale Bruce Hopkins says[18],

> When an organization scales, at some point, one needs to hire managers. Many people think of tentatively stepping in and having it as a part-time role. Don't do that. You are either not big enough to need managers or you are big enough to have dedicated managers.
>
> Be critical of your ideas. Of course, you want something to succeed, but if after a while something doesn't work out, it might be the plan and not the people.
>
> Most of the time, people fall under one of the two (manager/IC) because it is difficult to be good at both. Forcing them to do both will bring no success, and they will be inclined at most times to choose one over the other.
>
> Make sure to have realistic expectations that are communicated to team leads. An imposter syndrome is commonplace across the engineering world and when people are put into a new role, they will attribute all hardships to their own incompetence and not the inherent contradictions of the role.

Sorry, I've got some bad news. I've worked at a number of companies and asked around at a whole bunch more and the consistent response is: nobody trains you in how to be a manager. It gets worse. Those companies that do have training generally have useless training. Perhaps it's delivered by enthusiastic third-party suppliers, but is so devoid of content as to make it meaningless. Sometimes it's just access to a portal of online courses who earnestly

---

[18]https://www.platohq.com/articles/the-in-between-of-being-an-ic-and-a-manager-1125910140

tell you how to have difficult conversations. I shouldn't be too hard on employers, at least that is some kind of effort. And good manager training courses are hard to come up with.

There are a few exceptions – when I was working at Countdown in New Zealand, they had a management training course run by Jenny Gunn. I don't know whether it was the practicalities of running a team or how to be aware of problematic knee jerk answers to common questions, but it was universally agreed to be incredibly helpful. The funny thing was that it was available to all – junior analysts, team leaders and managers.

Most management training I've experienced has been focussed on the processes that involve the manager. Things like how to run a performance review – and sure, it's important to understand those practical elements of managerial tasks. But where good management training really proves itself is when it identifies the reality of critical conversation points that are surprisingly universal. Things like:

"Aaron, you have to get someone to check your code before committing it into the repo."

"But Babu doesn't."

Now, it's tempting to say, "I will talk to Babu," but that generates an obligation to tell Aaron about that conversation with Babu. You can expect Aaron to check in periodically enquiring whether you've had that conversation. You become beholden to Aaron. Not a good place to be. Instead, it's important to negate that whole conversation thread.

"I'm not talking about Babu. I'm talking to you about your behaviour. I need to see evidence of a senior developer checking your code prior to it going into the repo. That's part of our ways of working. Can you do that for me?"

And in the next team meeting. "Just a reminder about our process. After we've written up a piece of code and tested it locally, we must get a senior developer to check the code and sign off that it's performed as per spec and that they're happy for it to go live. Chen, what do we do if we can't find a senior developer? What's the escalation process?"

And that's exactly the sort of thing that Jenny's course covered.

And I'm not suggesting that there are no good management training courses, just that they are few and far between. Frequently, firms will provide some of the following, expecting that to tick the box of management training:

- Third party delivered courses that are really just a group session on, "What do you think you should do in this situation?"
- Unlimited access to a provider of online training courses.

How do you find a good training course? Well, you can't all get Jenny Gunn to run her course – she's got kids and lives in New Zealand, so you'll have to keep an ear to the ground about good management courses in your area and then press for them to be made available to you.

Expose the Data

The ability of stakeholders to consume the artefacts that you produce can be a little hit or miss. The data maturity of those stakeholders is one of the things you should be looking to increase. One of the dangerous attitudes that you can have is similar to the IC attitude towards the artefacts: that responsibility ends when they have been delivered.

It came up in conversation with one of my interviewees.

"So, what do you do when your team has created this brilliant dashboard and the stakeholder, who had pushed really hard for that to be the next thing built, doesn't bother to look at it?"

"I don't let that happen."

"What, you mean you check the usage stats afterwards? Holding them to account after the fact sounds dangerous, politically."

"That's because I didn't rely on them to check the numbers themselves. What I did was, I brought the data to them. That's the only way to bring value to the business. If they said they needed the data every week, I went to them and walked through the dashboard with them every week. And I helped them interpret the dashboard. Being there with them when they were looking at the dashboard certainly helped with finding the friction points to using the thing, but getting them to walk me through how they interpreted it and how they would change what they were doing off the back of it allowed me to get closer to the way they thought about the business. And that helped me to get the next levels of automation put into place: Email alerts for movements in metrics that they cared about and automated proactive insights based on what was in those dashboards. Once they learned they could trust the automated emails, they said that they didn't need some of those dashboards. The alerts short-cut that process and let them be confident that they were correctly monitoring the metrics that they cared about."

Exposing the data is important, but it can be taken too far: you must be careful to avoid the data-go-round. This occurs when you have a data-savvy stakeholder who needs data to do their work, but doesn't have the technical data engineering ability to get that data. In the worst example I've seen, a data engineer creates an automated workflow to extract data from the ERP and places the data into the data warehouse. That data is then ingested into a data visualisation system like Tableau. Then the stakeholder (in this case someone from accounting) goes to the dashboard and downloads the data into an Excel spreadsheet so that they can perform whatever manipulations or investigations on it. Now, there may very well be additional data that is enriching that original data feed from the ERP that the stakeholder needs and therefore this kind of makes sense. But the overheads and technical debt involved with maintaining a full pipeline for a single user's data needs always makes me wonder if there is a better solution to this use case.

It gets even more fun! I worked with a stakeholder who would have a data requirement but wanted various business rules baked into the ETL process – which staff member was responsible for a particular category of products, for example. Of course, the expectation was that whenever there was a change to those responsibilities that we would leap to alter the ETL code to map those responsibilities to the data. This wasn't acceptable and I very quickly put in place a mapping table in a spreadsheet that they had access to (this was the easiest way of eliciting data from the business: we weren't allowed a web-based front end for the data).

Whatever they put in that spreadsheet would be used for the responsibilities and it would only be accessed once when the ETL ran and if they didn't get the changes in before the daily ETL ran, then they would have to wait until the next day for that change to flow through the data. That worked reasonably well until the stakeholders messed with the format of the spreadsheet, which stopped the ETL from running. When they came to the team in panic we would shrug and say, "We told you not to change the column headings or the name of the sheets. If you change it back, it will work tonight, but we can't afford to drop everything and rerun the ETL just because you can't follow instructions." The only way we resisted the pressure from the stakeholders' senior managers was to refer to the numerous times they had made this sort of error and refer to the length of time that the ETL took to run. The reports would only be available at the end of the day, anyway, so they gained zero working hours if we lost hours of working time to fix their error.

One thing we perhaps should have done is introduced some code into that spreadsheet to make sure that the column headings and sheet name were never changed and that the file itself was not left open at the end of the day. All three happened at one time or another and all three caused the ETL process to fail. No ETL, no reporting.

CHAPTER 11

Structure

Imposter Syndrome (And How to Kill It)

If it's your first time as a manager, take a deep breath. Congratulations. It's an exciting time! But if you are anything like the first-time managers I've spoken to, there will be a little voice in your head (and with some people it's louder than with others) who will be saying, "You? A manager? Who do you think you are? You don't deserve to be a manager!" That nagging voice will spoil your experience as a new manager and may even drive you from the role if you let it. But I can help you kill that voice.

Let's talk about what that voice is: it's the manifestation of your anxiety and fears. It is self-talk and in this case it's very negative.

I want you to tell it the following (not out loud because we don't want to get you locked up). "I'm not a great manager *yet*. But I will be. It's unreasonable to think that I will be excellent straight away. So, I'm going to learn. It will take time."

This does two things. You're acknowledging the sliver of a fact that is driving those self-doubts. As a first-time manager, you probably aren't very good. But the most important thing is that you focus on the process of becoming better, rather than on where you are at the moment, and you answer the criticism while putting yourself in the best place to actually get better. You will not improve if you sit there and beat yourself up. Beating yourself up is a self-fulfilling prophecy.

And then, you must be humble. You won't know everything. You might not know how to handle difficult conversations. You're unlikely to know all the processes and HR rules from the managerial point of view. Do whatever course your employer offers. Ask your peers, ask your boss, ask HR for help. Don't be afraid to say things like, "I don't know what the policy is here for this, let me find that out and get back to you."

If you focus on the process of becoming a better manager rather on the fact that you've never done it before and have no idea what you are doing, then you are more likely to quieten that nagging little voice in your head.

One note about this: not knowing the correct actions according to the policy is one thing, but always remember you have a duty of care to your staff that comes above everything. If they are in physical or emotional danger, your immediate and obvious action should be to protect them or remove them from the dangerous situation. If your intention is pure, that should go a long way in defending those actions to senior management. Having pure intentions is not a "get out of jail free" card, but it should go a long way in your defence should push come to shove. Again, my lawyers would like me to point out that this is general guidance only and my publishers and I can't be held responsible for any adverse outcomes coming from following or partially following the recommendations in this text.

It's also natural to watch other managers and how they perform and use them to identify shortcomings in how you operate. Being brand new and having really good colleagues could lead you to focus on the gap between where they are and where you are. But it shouldn't. There's always something that you can learn from your peers and one of the best ways of improving is to ask people you admire for a coffee and then ask them questions like, "how did you work out how to handle <that awkward conversation that they aced>?" or, "How did you develop such a good relationship with <person in their team>?" Those conversations could very well develop into a mentoring relationship that we will cover in the next section.

A helpful action I would recommend when dealing with Imposter Syndrome is to recognise when you do something well. If appropriate, celebrate that in public. The reason I bring that up is that you must recognise when you have grown or developed in your skill set so that you fully appreciate the progress that you make. You probably have a checklist of "things that a good manager does" in your head. Ticking off each checkbox is a good way of making sure you're moving in that direction.

Lastly, it's really important to know that regardless of the support (or lack thereof) that you get from your employer, there are a lot of resources available on the web, and at least one of them is going to resonate with you. I have some links on the subject on the link page for this book on my website (see the appendix for the link), but you can get some really good resources merely by doing a search for "imposter syndrome" online.

Mentor Programs

One of the best things you can do as a brand-new manager is find a mentor. It doesn't matter if they are also employed by your company or whether they are external, the most important thing is that you can trust them. Some companies have formal mentor programs. In my experience it's good if these have a short commitment period – three months or so. This is so you can shop around and find the person at the right level who you can trust and who is committed to turning up and talking about the things you need to talk about. To prepare for these sessions it's a good idea to have a list of the issues that are top of mind for you. You should also write down all the parts of those issues so that you can lead the mentor through your thinking and the scenario so that they can come up with the right questions to tease out the facts and then give you the advice you're looking for. Sometimes, the process of clarifying the issue enough to be able to explain it to someone else is enough to give you an insight on how to proceed (it's called the Rubber Duck Debugging[19] theory in programming).

The best mentoring programs are actually "two up," which means that the mentor is two levels higher in the career ladder than the mentee. This means that the mentee is not a career challenger for the mentor and the mentor is close enough to the mentee that they can remember what it was like at that position, but far enough removed to have the perspective of knowing what is required to get to the next level. They can also prevent dead ends or bad choices because they have made the move that you will be looking to make next, and can tell you what they went through to get to where they are now.

Story time

A brand-new manager reached out to me to be her mentor. I was honoured and accepted, and then looked around the org and realised I was the only one of her peers who had been outside the org and had any sort of management experience, but it was still nice to be asked. Anyway, she came to me with a scenario.

---

[19]https://rubberduckdebugging.com/

When she had been a member of the team that she now managed, they had a particular project that always made her uncomfortable. It involved exposing client data to those clients so that they could make informed decisions. And we charged the clients for accessing that data. All permitted activities with actions consistent with the privacy policies, so no issues there. The issue was that the access management, the process whereby users were onboarded or offboarded, was a bolted-on task to one of the analysts in the team. IT did not want to support the system and hated the fact that we were shipping data out of our data lake. IT had also been told in the past that we would not generate revenue from the service, and they had had to poke a hole in the firewall to make it all work – and most importantly, it had been running off someone's laptop. In fact, to say that IT wasn't happy that this "side of the desk" project had suddenly had revenue implications and was something that people were relying on, was an understatement.

The new manager came to me and said, "This feels really uncomfortable. I know that my previous boss had also felt uncomfortable but whenever they had raised those feelings with the stakeholder and our senior management, they had been overruled. Or if not overruled, they'd be given platitudes because no one wants to piss off the stakeholder."

"The stakeholder who is receiving the revenue for providing the service? It goes on their P&L?"

"Yes."

"OK, so you've identified a whole bunch of risks, and these are looking like they are sitting on your head at the moment, regardless of whether your predecessor raised them or not. The fact that you're getting platitudes means that you or your previous manager have not succeeded in getting our senior management to appreciate the enormity of the situation. We need to act quickly to itemise those risks and get the right people to treat these risks as theirs rather than yours."

We went through each of the risks and identified who should best be dealing with them and why, and then I instructed her to go up our chain of command.

It turned out that while the fact that there were unmitigated risks was raised with our senior management, nobody had itemised the details of the risks and their possible outcomes, and called out who was best placed to mitigate those risks. The ramifications had never been spelled out and so there was no real understanding of just how much was at stake. And so, nothing was done about it. Because we had identified the obvious owners of each of the risks, the analytics senior management were very happy with raising the situation with those responsible heads, because they didn't have to actually do anything except follow up with them later. And because the new manager had all her facts in a row and had escalated, she looked great. Having someone to run things past is a good way to check what your gut is telling you. And it's always handy to have a second opinion on the method of delivering this information.

Reverse Mentoring

I've not done reverse mentoring but it's when you get direct feedback from one of your direct reports about how you are coming across and how the team is reacting to the things you are trying to say. This can be difficult because you are putting the reverse mentor in an awkward position that they might say something indelicate that could anger you, so it's vital to develop trust and create a relationship with them so they can trust that you will not take offence at what they say. The process of doing this will also allow your mentor to see you as open to feedback and therefore vulnerable and interested in developing and improving.

I shouldn't have to tell you this, but make sure you have a filter on what you admit to with the reverse mentor. Breaking down in tears as you sob about how taking the manager role was a mistake and that you don't know what you are doing will not endear yourself to any team members!

Protect The Team

A big part of the job of manager is to protect the team. Sometimes that is from stakeholders, sometimes from senior management, and sometimes from the business as a whole. Let me explain.

It's possible that your stakeholders are perfect. That they have all their requirements for the year lined up, they know their objectives and how they fit into the wider objectives of the business. They know what they want analytics to do, and they have figured out which pieces of work they want done in which order and what the relative business value of each is. They are available to the analytics team so that the team can learn what drives them and their pain points. And they know that analytics is trying to help them, so they are friendly and happy and kind, and everyone works together towards common goals. And they know that a certain amount of the analytics team's time will be required for admin, refactoring and forcibly retiring artefacts and workflows that are no longer needed. It is possible that you work in such an environment. But... it's unlikely.

There will be some part of that relationship with one or other of the stakeholders that is not perfect. And that could be different for each combination of team member and stakeholder. So, you will have to figure out where the issue is and how you propose to mitigate it. It might not be possible to fix the situation and so you might simply have to insert yourself in some way to make it as good as you can get it. Some examples of this include when a stakeholder is constantly interrupting the team (possible solution: we now have a non-contact Tuesday and Wednesday to allow the team to get really deep into the work), or where one particular stakeholder has a prickly personality (possible solution: it might be a good idea if two of the team are on these calls). Of course, sometimes you need to escalate.

Likewise, there can be a lot of things going on at the senior manager or manager level that don't need to impact the team. A director of risk management for the US division wants to consolidate the analytics teams into the Reporting Department. This will be a six-month process and because of the politics between the VP of the US division and the VP of the EMEA division, it's unlikely to go ahead. Why would you worry the team with that sort of "maybe" or "possible" thing that has a horizon measured in years? You are certainly the conduit for communicating what the team needs to know, but concentrating on only what is important allows the team to focus.

It might take a while to learn where that line is drawn, but letting the team have the headspace to do their work can be incredibly valuable.

Structural Failures

What are structural failings? A better question might be, "Why are there so few good managers?"

Well, you've got ambitious people who excel at the technical parts of their job and who want to achieve, and you identify the things that they have to achieve and behaviours that they need to exhibit in order to be eligible for the next step. And you promote them. And then you don't support these people in their new roles. You don't train properly.

They turn into uber-analysts because they can't delegate and do everything themselves because that's the thing that they know how to do, and they burn out. They work ridiculous hours to avoid drowning. They do not grow the team. They do not put time into the relationships with their stakeholders.

They run from emergency to emergency and very quickly exhaust themselves before they have the opportunity to grow their management muscles. No wonder so many people have horror stories about their managers!

Going Outside

I have come to the conclusion that whenever there is a manager role that becomes available and the company decides to go outside instead of promoting someone internally, what the managers making that decision are admitting is that, "We do not think that anyone we have, plus whatever added support we can provide, will compare with what an outsider has learned from their time as a manager elsewhere."

You could interpret this as a failure of the career growth systems, or perhaps an indication that none of the staff are currently ready. But I suspect it's the recognition that the business is not able to add sufficient support to get any of the current staff to the point where they might be able to perform as a manager.

What If It Doesn't Work Out?

I spoke to someone who was a senior manager, and she was miserable. She had a team that she was managing, there were personal objectives that had to be delivered and she was running from one emergency to another. She looked around and wondered why she was so miserable – this was what she had aspired to for so long, but the reality of the role was nothing like what she expected. She had no reflecting time, no time to learn, no time to be human or to metabolise life. On the face of it she was performing well – but she felt like no one could see that below the water she was paddling like crazy.

She spoke with her boss, and they went through the options. She could go down to three days a week, but that wouldn't help much because the firm would have to hire another manager and the nature of the work that she was doing wouldn't shift enough to make a difference to her psyche. Another manager also meant more cost for the business.

The boss could see that she was at risk of attrition and so suggested a different option. The part of the work that she was enjoying was the senior IC work – leading engagements and delivering to clients. So, the goal was to keep that part, and to offload the line responsibility for her team to a different manager. Now, the nature of work is that it will fill whatever time you assign to it, so in order to guarantee that she had time to learn and to decompress and to achieve a thrive state she went down to four days a week. I asked her if she had to take a twenty percent drop in salary and she smiled and said that with her performance being so good and her raise, she only had to take a fifteen percent drop in pay.

Other firms offer a form of "try before you buy," in which as a senior IC you take on the line management of one of the more junior analysts. This allows you to determine whether being a manager is for you and starts the ball rolling on learning how to be a good manager. By only taking one direct report it also allows you to prevent becoming overwhelmed with the volume of pastoral care that is required when you manage staff.

Other firms divorce the line management trial entirely from the hierarchy so that the risk of being bad at it is removed from the consideration for promotion. It's important to periodically check in to make sure things are progressing agreeably.

It's really important to me that you know that there are ways of improving as a manager. It's also vitally important to me that you know that if you are not enjoying yourself and you've tried everything, that there are other options available.

CHAPTER 12

Problems, So Many Problems

Here are some concrete problems I've encountered (or heard about) and how I handled it. Or maybe how I wished I had handled it. Or maybe how other people handled it.

Going Straight to the Team

If one of your stakeholders gets into the habit of going straight to your team to give them tasks, then it is symptomatic of a bad relationship. And that relationship is with you. You have some options:

Have a word. You have to bring this behaviour up with the stakeholder and express how and why it is wrong. My experience is that this will not work, because they already know it's the wrong thing to do, and they have still done it. But you have to lay the groundwork for escalation and that is to document the meeting and identify their reasons.

You then counter with the fact that it either drives the team to do additional work, which is not acceptable because it leads to burn out, or else results in them having to drop something else. This puts deadlines at risk. Which deadlines? I'm sorry, you don't get to prioritise the team's workload, that's my job. And I won't allow someone else to jeopardise my team's targets. You're putting my bonus at risk.

Then, you will have to bring this up with your boss. That's only fair because you need to let them know of potential issues – and this is a big one. If they are onside, then you can both go to the perpetrator's boss to explain the behaviour and ramifications.

You also have to have conversations with your team. It's very common for them not to feel comfortable or confident enough to push back on sideways asks.

Coach the team on what to say.

They should be able to say something like, "Sure, I can do this, but it will put my achievables at risk and therefore I need to know my manager and stakeholders have signed off on this change in my priorities. Have you spoken to them?"

If the stakeholder says, "Oh go on, it will only take x amount of time."

Your team member can say, "I'm sorry, we're behind already and the length of time that a task takes is not something you decide. And the context-switching time is not trivial. Swapping back and forwards between projects derails both projects."

It will take multiple occasions to ensure the behaviour changes. Be sure to maintain a paper trail of all the times that they ask and what the team was working on when they were interrupted.

Ask questions like, "It has come to my attention that you are going directly to Uday to ask for work to be done when we have an onboarding process that should be followed. Do we need a refresher on how that works? Is there an issue with the process?"

Playing dumb is a way for them to express dissatisfaction with the process if that is where the issue lies, but also gives them an out because it's no longer about them.

If their issue is that their work is not being prioritised and they are frustrated about this, then that's an argument for a resourcing discussion. "It sounds like this project is very important to you and you really need it to happen, but because this person and that person have prioritised this task and that task, that means you're going to have to wait until this date before we can even start this job. Is it worth talking to this stakeholder to free up some of our time to get you something quick and dirty? You should probably have a solid business case behind you there – I know that this stakeholder has targets of $4M in mind for the work he's proposing we do for him."

My Team

But what if your boss tries to manage your team? You might have to take them to one side and have a little word, whether it's as soon as possible after the intervention or as soon as you find out about it. It's important that you do it as soon as possible either way, so as to not allow the behaviour to continue. The reasoning is that you are responsible for the allocation of the team's time and that everything should come through you. Most importantly, it confuses your team when the responsibility for their prioritisation is muddled.

So, how do you tell your boss off? It's important to be respectful, but to let them know in no uncertain terms that their interference is not welcome or warranted and won't be tolerated. Asking if they want to swap roles, while passive aggressive, should put them in their place because it identifies that your role is the one with the team management component and that they are the one playing in your space, rather than the other way around. It's also a possible indication that the senior manager is potentially a micromanager or a meddler, and you don't want those.

Stakeholders Wanting Their Own Analytic Team

Quite frequently you will find that there is a very thin line between the work that you and your team do in analytics and the work that your stakeholder does. This is especially true when you both have skills and access to the same tool. This situation inevitably throws up its own set of unique issues. One of those will be discussed in the Unpopular Ideas section (How Long?), but here are some other considerations that have come up with my interviewees.

One interviewee related the experience of having a stakeholder who had managed to get a single analytics resource and insisted on assigning them tasks directly. They did not want them to be in the pool of analysts in the team, they wanted them to only work on their tasks, and the stakeholder would handle all the non-pastoral care elements of the management role.

The obvious shortcoming of that situation was that the interviewee couldn't follow the progress of the analyst through their tasks or know how well they were delivering because they weren't having regular check-ins. The interviewee rolled their eyes. "That's not the worst part. They want total control over the analyst but they also insist on having someone fill in for them when they are away on holiday or out sick."

"That doesn't sound right to me," I told them. "If they have one analyst, then they get them for 52 weeks of five days, so 260 days, less their personal holidays (25 in that country) plus bank holidays

(8). So, they only get them for 227 days – fewer if they're ill. That's all that the funding for one analyst per year covers."

"Nope. They want to have a continual resource available to them and that's 260 days."

That level of unreasonableness can be matched by a different stakeholder in the same firm who wanted to create their own artefacts using the data visualisation tool that the analytics team used, and then have the analytics team take over the support function for those artefacts. The argument there was that the stakeholder with the artefact generating skill was getting the results that they needed but then the "boring parts" could be taken by the analytics team.

The interviewee shook their head. "I didn't have enough political capital to fight that because it sounds like a reasonable request, right? All we need to do is "finish it off." But this was a terrible situation because we had no control over the quality of the work that they were doing, we had no insight into what business question they were trying to answer and whether it was even a good approach to answering that question. Most importantly, those tasks were poison to the team because it removed any satisfaction from the analyst who was polishing someone else's work until it fit all the governance steps that the team had to comply with."

"That sounds terrible, how did you fix that situation?"

"Initially I told the stakeholders that it was ok as long as we had those artefacts given to us and that they complied with our standards and governance steps, but they never did because those steps only applied when you were productionising the artefact generation. So, things like code reviews, query efficiency, ensuring accessibility, those sorts of things were not done and we would end up with a limp salad. And how could anyone take pride in releasing something like that when they couldn't say for sure that it was fit for purpose, because they didn't know what it was supposed to do or how well it did it?"

"So, what did you do?"

"In the end I had to tell the stakeholder that we wouldn't be able to take on any of those pre-prepared artefacts, but that we could take them as a Proof of Concept to illustrate the sort of thing that they were after. We were clear with them that they would still have to spell out exactly what they were after, what the business problem was, that sort of thing, so it wouldn't really be too much of a shortcut, but what it would do was prevent any of the situations when what we delivered wasn't exactly what they were after."

"And how did they handle that? Did they accept that solution?"

"Not really. They hated it, but my team was much happier with it. And eventually the analytics team started to demonstrate the improvements on the original artefacts so that the stakeholders could see the value added by the analytics team. But there was a while there when the head stakeholder would be reaming me because we were double-handling the work that had already been 'mostly' done by their team."

Barriers to Success?

Shouldn't the business set you up for success?

I was asked this once by someone who had decided to opt out of the rat race and was now a freelancer. It is easy for the people management side of things to be lost when the manager has too many direct reports and their own deliverables. So, if you were faced with the choice of spending time delivering what your boss can see and will ask you about, or spending time with your team who are capable of doing the work that you give them, which do you think will attract the energy of the manager? I'm not asking what should happen, but merely demonstrating the choice that is generally made, and why. Unless the business is interested in measuring the manager's performance by considering the management of their team, they will ignore how well they grow their team members and focus on their deliverables. The best places I have worked are interested in "what" you achieved throughout the year, but also "how" you achieved it.

One interviewee even suggested that it was easy to be a great boss because, "Standards are so low that by just showing up and managing the sprawl you prove your value to the business."

Employees Quit Managers

Ever wonder why job ads focus on perks? I don't mean the salary, but all the other bits – the "cultural" things: Dress down Fridays, table tennis table, pizza parties, etc.

These are easy to arrange, cheap to implement and are seen as moving the needle with regards to motivation. They don't though: motivation is better built up through interaction with the manager (Frederick Herzberg in HBR Sep/Oct 1987[20]). But the job advert can't promise a great manager – the employer can't promise the sort of things that lead directly to highly engaged employees. These can only be delivered by messy humans. Managers. You.

And as we've discussed, there is usually little support for new managers to gain those skills. So, a manager can either develop those skills and continue on their career to senior management, or take a little longer to develop those skills. But they remain a

---

[20]https://www.indeed.com/career-advice/career-development/herzberg-theory

manager during that time, trying to make their way. And when you think back on your career, how many of your managers would you consider "good?" Laurence J. Peter came up with the Peter Principle[21], which says that people rise to their level of incompetence. You can see how it happens. "Zain, you're good at making dashboards, we'll promote you. Oh, you don't seem to be performing as a manager. Well, we can give you access to this online resource to try and make you better." In the meantime, the team isn't getting good management. Everybody has a story about a bad manager!

So, here is the problem. You have to develop a healthy distance between yourself and the team so that you won't be devastated if one of your team leaves. Especially if they leave because of you. And there is a pretty good chance that in the early days at least, when you are not a good manager, one or more of your team will leave because of you. And you need to be able to insulate yourself from the feelings of guilt that are generated by someone leaving their job because you cannot give them what they need in terms of being a good manager, while you furiously and relentlessly attempt to develop the skills that you need.

You need to tell yourself that the only thing you can control are your attempts to improve. And you have to be ok with that, because guess what? You will never know the reason someone *really* leaves their job. Some may tell you to be hurtful. Some may not tell you to spare your feelings. And you may feel so guilty that you aren't performing as well as you would like that even if they are not leaving because of you, you think that they are. "What if the dream job on the other side of the country that's so much closer to their significant other and paying twice as much is really just an excuse to get away from me and my trainee manager skill set?"

---

[21]https://en.wikipedia.org/wiki/Peter_principle

That's the curse of the manager role: you will never know the truth about what people think about you or why they are really leaving. You have to concentrate on what you can control and ignore everything else. It's tough. But the extra money that comes with the manager job title comes with that catch.

Where Now?

The promotion from IC to manager is probably the biggest hurdle that you will face in your career. But after you've quietened the imposter syndrome, figured out how to carve out time to think strategically and have managed to have good relationships with your stakeholders, it may be time to start thinking about your next step: the senior manager.

I asked one of my interviewees about that next step, from manager to senior manager. He's a straight talker and leaned back from the table and thought for a second.

"If you want to be promoted, you have to be the obvious choice. Even before the vacancy is announced you have to be who people are thinking about when they think about you and your peers. They have to know your name, they have to have an opinion on you and your work, so they not only have to have heard of you, but they also have to have a favourable opinion about what you can do, or ideally had some first-hand experience of the value that you bring."

Whenever this guy got talking it was like a train going downhill – slowly at first and then as he warmed to the subject he would get faster and faster.

"You need to understand that the role of manager and senior manager are different from your Individual Contributor and have a different skill set. It is increasingly relevant for those in leadership roles to know how to talk to people and how to navigate conflict. It becomes less about what you know and more about who you are – a huge part is about personality. You need to know how to talk, how to listen, how to understand a problem and most importantly, how to answer the question. You also need to be relevant, whether that is internally or externally, perhaps speaking at conferences and being a "thought leader." You also have to manage expectations – I had a stakeholder wanting something at the end of Friday and so I asked if they would be doing anything over the weekend with the results and they said no, so I said I'd have it ready first thing Monday."

So that's one option: senior manager. But if you have done some time as a manager and you don't fancy the people management side of things, does that make you a failure? No! In fact, if you reach that conclusion then that's brilliant. It means you know what works for you and for whatever reason, being a people manager is not what floats your boat. That's good. Because now you can focus on moving your career in a direction that will maximise the chances of you being happy.

I'll tell you this: if the only reason you are in a manager role is because that's the only step on the career ladder available to you, then you won't feel fulfilled and it's likely you won't develop those skills you need to be a good manager very quickly – if at all. This means your team will suffer.

If that's the case for you, do me a favour. If your employer does not have an IC role at the manager level, have a word with your bosses and see if there is appetite for creating one. Or find an employer who has one. Or find a role with the name of manager but without direct reports. Or if you are brave enough and have enough contacts who can give you contracts, go out freelancing or contract working. Being highly paid for your deep technical knowledge is another way of making sure you are moving forward.

Think about it: why are there so many bad managers? And what is the effect on the team if they have a bad manager? And where do you sit in that equation? Are you someone who is going to stay as a mediocre manager, doing a bad job for your team because you like the extra money and have no other options? Are you going to be the manager who continually learns and improves?

PART 6

Guidance for Senior Managers

Depending on the organisation you work for, a senior manager could have any number of titles – here's a bunch of them. Associate Director, Director, Senior Director, Head of Analytics, CDO (Chief Data Officer), CAO (Chief Analytics Officer), or even just Senior Manager. Whatever they're called, these positions sit between the people or person in charge of the business and those who manage the people doing the work. Depending on the size of the analytics function, they tend to manage other people managers, but of course in organisations that are particularly flat, elements of what they do may indeed be shared among the few that there are in analytics. Likewise, the number of these roles increases as the size and bureaucracy of the business increases.

Fundamentally, the senior manager understands the connection between analytics and where the business or a unit wants to move strategically. They have to know where their team will fit in, and how to make themselves indispensable. They need to be ambitious and have an idea of how they will be useful and find fame.

It's essential to be a creator of value, not just cost centre delivery mechanism.

CHAPTER 13

Getting Good

How Did I Get Here?

It was probably more money. It might have also been for more of a challenge, more responsibility, to exercise different skills or to further one's career.

The first step is the firm agreeing that they need someone in that role. Then you have to be the best person in contention for that role. The advice and commentary in the Guidance for Manager section applies here also. But the senior manager role comes with its own additional nuance. You see, when you work as an IC and to some extent as a manager, you get the job based on evidence of potential performance in the role: what you *might* be like. But at the senior manager level there is much more focus on what you have done. Therefore, there has to be enough of a trail of successful performance in similar roles to justify your position as a senior manager.

There is a little bit of the same protectionism that you see in the step from IC to manager in the step from manager to senior manager. You need the experience in the job to show that you can do it, which does not help you when you're applying for that first job. That can be frustrating – a catch 22 where you need experience to get the job but without the job you can't get the experience! Once you do break into the senior management roles, you'll be glad of that requirement because that will help protect you a little from your competition. Because at this level there are significantly fewer roles.

So, how do you differentiate yourself from others going for that role? You really have to focus on the impact your efforts have on the business. You have to highlight the evidence that demonstrates you can do the job – even while you are not necessarily being paid to do it. And the evidence that you must show is different from that of the manager role.

Do I Have to Have Been an Analyst?

No. Of course, it would help if you had technical skills, as it would give you an instant boost in gravitas. But depending on the skills you do have and what you are being asked to do, it may not be necessary for you to have done what your team can do. The important thing to remember is the line, "I'm not being paid to do what you do; I'm being paid to do what I do."

One particular person springs to mind when talking about this point. I was talking to a senior manager in analytics and was looking at their LinkedIn profile as part of the pre-interview research. Puzzled, I asked them to talk me through how they happened to lead that function. They laughed and said that they didn't think that they would be able to tell me much about how to get promoted in an analytics org because they had come into the job sideways.

They had had a history of being awesome at managing accounts in the sales part of the business, had a wealth of experience in the industry, and had done more and more work with the data science and analytics team, so they knew what those teams were doing and where their value lay. The opportunity arose to harness that business value and gain more recognition for that work.

She began advocating for the team and had a few conversations with the CEO, ultimately managing to get them to agree to her taking over the team. I probed deeper because from what we had spoken about, I couldn't see how they could justify her position.

It turned out that there was a bit of a vacuum between the business and the analytics team in terms of defining the work that was required: the team was not producing quite the right insights because they did not understand the industry well enough to contextualise the tasks that they were getting. So, the senior manager was able to unlock their abilities by flavouring the task definitions with the industry knowledge that she had. She didn't need to talk about random forests or linear regressions to add value. She just had to let them know the reasoning behind the task and also the next aspect to look into to really move the needle for the business. She could see the highlights that looked interesting from the initial cut of data and could fill in the gaps where the definitions of the task perhaps weren't as well defined as they could have been.

That by itself would have justified the role, but she also was able to use her connections in the sales part of the business to promote the work that team did. Exposing the team's work to the rest of the senior managers was essential to unlocking the business value that they could generate. And the fact that she wouldn't get bogged down in the technical discussion of the delivery meant that she could focus on telling people about the business value.

She was also able to protect the team from unreasonable requests from other parts of the business because she had a more dispassionate view of what the team could do. I'm definitely not suggesting that everyone can make a good senior manager in the analytics area; there are numerous stories of senior managers from an IT or Finance background making a meal out of running analytics teams, but it is possible.

How to Excel

The internal conflict for the IC is that they want to play with the tools, but the business wants them to know their business area better than their stakeholder. Their horizon is behind them. The events that are stored as data that drive their insights are historical.

The internal conflict for the manager is that they fight fires that they know how to do, rather than taking a minute to think strategically. Their horizon stretches from the now to a few steps in front of them. They are moving from interacting with tools to interacting with Stakeholders.

The internal conflict for the senior manager is that they're coming across psychopaths and are usually not given support to deal with them. Their horizon is a year or more away. They're being asked to consider the answers to the question of, "So what?" Business knowledge is replaced with a crystal ball.

One of the points that continually came up in my interviews was that when the business is doing well, it's a totally different situation than when there is a downturn in business performance.

In a well-run company there is a very clear narrative: it is very clear what winning looks like. In a well-run company, they are very good at breaking the strategy down into components and delivering against that shared view. The CEO is ruthless in checking in so that every executive is held accountable for their part. As described to me:

What makes the top companies operate at the highest level? They are exceptional operators. They are clear on objectives and playing their position. (I had asked them a question about how to handle relationships at the senior level) And so there really isn't much friction there – everyone knows the plan, knows what they need to deliver and how that interfaces with the other members of the team.

But when things don't go so well, that's when things get tumultuous: everyone has a plan for how to save the day. And when everybody is looking around for the solution, they start pointing fingers and have plans that muddy borders.

So, your success at a deteriorating company will look totally different than at a company on an uptick. But there is something that should be the same in either environment.

The big difference between being a manager and a senior manager is that you are moving even further away from technology, and more towards psychology. Don't get me wrong, you're expected to have an intelligent insight into the pros and cons of the different technical products being considered for adoption, but the opportunities for hands-on coding diminish significantly.

So, what do you need to be able to do? Aside from the coaching and pastoral care of the manager role, there are also the interactions with more senior stakeholders, who may include the CEO. You will need to do more and more storytelling and build a narrative about where things are and where they are going. You may need to challenge the CEO.

The advice I was able to on this topic suggested that you have to put data behind the challenge and make it dispassionate. At that level you're usually hired based on how easy people think it will be to get along with you. So, you will have to finesse some tricky conversations. One way is to play to people's egos. When you are giving context for a discussion, you can say things like, "You'll recall that…" which implies that you don't need to tell them the background because they're so clued up, but that you will just for the sake of clarity. It's also a good idea to use non-aggressive language.

Storytime I

It can be a very tricky conversation is when a whole business unit is not performing and a hard discussion needs to take place. You wouldn't think that this would fall under the purview of a senior manager within analytics, but sometimes the analytics role is coupled with other parts of the business – sometimes Strategy, Product or Go to Market.

Go to Market is the part of the business that figures out how new products should be released and monetised. One senior manager told me about having to have a sensitive conversation when a new product wasn't working out. They were having to talk to the leader of the team that was trying to sell the new product and they weren't hitting their targets.

"Wow, so how did you have that conversation? Surely that would have been very difficult?"

"Yeah, it was – and one of the first things I did was to acknowledge that. I said to them, 'Hey, I can see that this conversation is going to have a huge personal impact on you, but we have to discuss the performance over the last six months and what we're going to do about it.'"

"How did they handle that?"

"They weren't stupid. They could see the writing on the wall. They knew the conversation was coming."

"What else did you say? How did you handle it?"

"I kept everything really factual. I didn't use language that assigned the blame to them personally. It was all, 'the product has not found the sales levels that we forecast' and, 'what activities have you got planned for the team to try to turn that around?' And a lot of, 'What do you need from me to help?' "

"So, what was the story, was it a bad launch? Not enough marketing? Something wrong with the internal processes to support the roll out?"

"In a way it doesn't matter, those are all excuses that they could use to try to say that it wasn't their fault, but the purpose of the meeting was not to apportion blame, it was to see if we could recover and most importantly where we needed to place our efforts. In that way I was able to wear my analytics hat to see what reporting or insights could help."

I found myself wondering if that sort of analytics support might have been better put in place from the start and my body language must have given me away.

"Oh no, they had all the analytics support they needed: all the metrics were defined and we were monitoring everything that needed monitoring even from before the launch. When I was asking if there was anything else he needed – that's code to say that if there were any future discussions with HR then I could say that I offered continual support. It's not really me offering anything – it's me protecting myself from fallout later on if things turn sticky."

So, here's the takeaway from that story: a lot of the time as a senior manager you are recognizing the potential outcomes from conversations and scenarios, and manoeuvring so that disaster is averted – or mitigating the risk should the situation take a turn for the worse.

Storytime II

In FMCG you have a hierarchy built primarily around the physical stores. The larger the store the more the kudos for running them. And their bosses aggregated the ego from all the stores in their capture area. Some of these store directors had salaries higher than the Prime Minister, and a corresponding level of ego. For anyone in analytics, dealing with that would be difficult, but one senior manager told me how he did it.

They had to persuade a particular store director to change their way of thinking. So, they took the long view and spent time with them on their turf. They made a point of visiting the store director's stores with them on their regular routes, attending their store manager meetings, and presenting with them. It was a good ego boost for them to have a head office person come along and talk to their team, it demonstrated that they were important and that they had attention from head office. Spending time together grew the relationship, and allowed the store director to recognise that the analytics senior manager was not a threat to them, but was there to help him look good in front of his troops.

The other prong to this approach was also to gain time with the store director's boss. By improving that relationship, the senior manager was able to determine how best to align his approach, prior to needing to push his agenda. I also think this was a good strategy to protect the analytics senior manager if the relationship with the store director started to falter; getting ahead of that message is a good idea. By ensuring that the message from analytics to the store director matched with what the store director was being told by his boss, it maximised the chance of it being listened to.

The analytics senior manager continued in their discussion of how to handle work relationships. Each person has one of three motivators: emotional, political and rational. Once you know which is predominant, you can address their concerns and couch your message in terms that they are more likely to be receptive to. You will need to make sure that the person trusts that you won't expose them, or make them look stupid, or selfish.

Storyteller

I mentioned in the chapter on IC that you need to become a storyteller – and that is true, but the hypothetical split of your time shown below may not match the reality of what you see around you in your workplace.

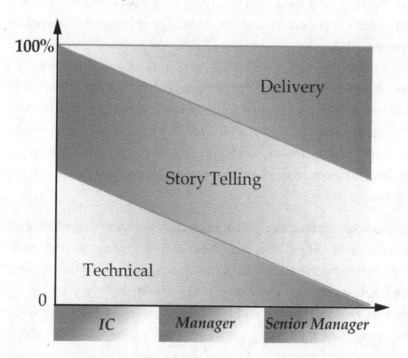

Figure 7 Different skills for different roles

Particularly in businesses where there is a vested interest in claiming credit for work done (and therefore the revenue this brings in), you may well see the proportion between delivery (the actual work done) and storytelling (claiming credit for the work done) fluctuate away from the proportion suggested above.

Let's break it down.

As a senior manager you have what is described in Michael Lewis' book Liar's Poker[22] as being the warm-up lap and the victory lap. This is when you go around the houses telling people what you will be delivering, and then after the fact you go back around and tell them what happened. You get in front of people twice. I've spoken to people about the proportion of time they spend doing one or other at the senior level and it's a good indicator that while it's all sales, it's vacuous when all your time is spent telling the story of what you've done while not actually undertaking the delivery. In fact, you probably have some idea of the proportion of storytelling to delivery that everyone in your peer group represents. Likewise, look back to the start of your career and see how you have changed over time.

One particular interviewee illustrated this by saying that when they started at their Big 4 firm that they were 5/95: that is, they were terrible at doing the story telling part and really good at the delivery part (they started as a manager). They said that they ended up closer to 30/70 at the end, and that they were frustrated that people who were more than 30% storytellers were promoted above them. This is understandable, as anyone doing the actual work does not want to be rewarding the people who are just doing the story telling. In fact, the worst person is the 100/0 – the person who comes

---

[22]https://www.amazon.com/dp/B09QY1QV4X

along and claims all the credit for the work but does no delivery. The frustrating thing is that they rise to a point – at which they are found out, but are still seen as successful.

If you are not a good storyteller, how do you get better? How do you go from a 5/95 to a 30/70? One way is to find someone who is closer to the inverse of where you want to be: in this case someone who is still delivering, but is still much better than you at the storytelling, and make sure you learn from them. A 5/95 working with a 70/30 will get you to a 30/70. It will rub off – as long as you are legitimately working with each other and not just delegating the storytelling part of the work. Other ways of growing that storytelling ability include joining external organisations like Toastmasters, taking courses, or trying stand up at an open mic night.

Funding / Costs / Revenue

One facet of the senior manager role within analytics that is not usually focussed on, is how analytics itself is funded. I spoke to one senior manager who stood out because they were adamant that analytics would not be a cost centre, but rather would pay its own way. I hadn't come across that and dove a little deeper. It turns out that the senior manager was not happy being beholden to other parts of the business for funding, and so decided to turn their knowledge of their customers into products that the business could sell. Note that I said that it was the knowledge of their customers that led to the product development? That's the opposite of how I understood commercialisation of data – turns out that I was wrong.

One of the benefits of working in an agency is that your stakeholders are your customers. As you grow your knowledge of their business, you get the opportunity to wow them with additional insights and that makes your relationship stickier and reduces their propensity to churn. It also allows a more in-depth knowledge of their pain points. This then allows you to look around at the data that you are sitting on and come up with solutions for those problems. In this case, the product was something that could be resold multiple times to all the participants in the market, which made it a very lucrative new product indeed, and allowed that senior manager to link the additional revenue to their team size and ultimately led to control of their own destiny.

Not all of us work in businesses that have external customers who could lead to additional revenue streams, although I think at a certain point you should be thinking in those terms anyway. If you can get close enough to your customers and learn their pain points and appetite to pay to have those pain points addressed, you can be justified in looking internally to see what data is available to solve those pain points. Capturing that additional business value, whether it is from internal stakeholders or someone willing to actually pay money, is definitely worth pursuing.

One thing we all share is a pressure to reduce costs. Consider the history of moving data into the cloud.

Initially the argument was made that we should move our data into the cloud because it was cost effective; the comparison of cloud storage to the hassle and capital expenditure of owning data centres and the hardware within them meant that it was an easy sell. Sure, there were issues with privacy and jurisdictions, but by and large those issues were addressed and the world moved on. The vendors themselves promoted the notion that everything should be put into the cloud, and to somewhat soften the blow the cloud providers offered various price points for data depending on how frequently you needed access.

Cloud-first became a buzzword, and some big corporates made a point of making every department put all their data into the cloud. They would then have committees that would operate governance functions to approve each of these cloud migrations, which would lead to the Kafkaesque experience of one part of the business saying that everything had to be on the cloud and another part saying that your particular bit of data was not allowed to be on the cloud and somehow you ended up looking from one to the other saying, "I don't care where this data is actually stored but one or other of you is going to be very cross with me in a potentially career limiting way and I don't feel very empowered in the discussions."

Anyway, with all legacy data moving to the cloud and any new products having to have their data natively stored in the cloud, you can see how the IT team's budgets can get out of date very quickly. The amounts spent on storage were a lot more at the end of the year than at the beginning, and the only saving grace was that IT was bearing the cost of it rather than analytics – and you should thank whatever deity you pray to that analytics doesn't report to IT (and apologies if it does where you work!!).

Additionally, in a lot of cases the processing of the data was also moved into the cloud, so the raw data was stored in the cloud, a cloud-based aggregation was run and then the results of that aggregation were also stored in the cloud. If there was no governance process keeping an eye on any duplicated effort in the different teams within analytics, it was very easy for the same data in the same aggregations built by different teams to incur double or triple the expense in the cloud. And of course, there was the compute cost as well as the storage costs!

One of the reasons I promoted the idea of a network diagram that showed the data all the way from source to how many times the dashboards were accessed, was to make sure that you had visibility of all the processing, all of the aggregations, all the potential duplicates and most importantly, which things can be switched off. One thing I haven't done is attach a dollar amount to each of the items in the network diagram, but that would be an interesting process to identify which items incur which cost, and to ensure that any piece of analytics work generates a business value that justifies its existence. Very few analytics organisations do this, which is a pity, because having a whole department who are interested in keeping discipline on which datasets get stored is much better than just one manager running around trying to tell people "no." In Lauren Balik's[23] words:

> Ensure that data team individual contributors have access to understanding the fiscal impact of building the nth pipeline or writing additional SQL.

---

[23]https://medium.com/@laurengreerbalik

CHAPTER 14

The Psychopath

The ability of the senior manager to influence others is one of the most prominent requirements in job ads, and I've explained some of the methods of achieving that, above. However, I'd now like to highlight where I've seen a lot of brand-new senior managers falter in their career in analytics.

Imagine, you start your career because you like a particular tool. You get good at it and then discover that real career success comes from learning about the actual business unit that you support, rather than how good you are with the tool. So, you learn more about the business and discover that you like that, and you do well enough to be promoted to manager. After thrashing around trying to do all the work and working eighty-hour weeks, you figure out how to arrange your team so that they can do the work and you can a) look after them, b) control the flow of work through the team and c) have some time to think strategically. You manage to get really close to your stakeholders and drive some really important changes that they had not thought of, that have huge positive impacts on the business unit.

Let's think about the people that you've dealt with. Your team has been other analytics folk and you know them and get along with them because you share an outlook on work and life, and they're your people. You get along with your stakeholders because of your shared focus on making their team better and your shared understanding of the problems that they face, plus the possible solutions. And so, you naturally get another promotion and now you deal with senior management. Everyone you've dealt with up to that point you have understood. You share their values and their problems, and you can work with them because you understand them.

But at senior manager level you discover one of two things:

Either the company that you work for somehow epitomises a psychopath, or else you literally start working with someone who is a psychopath. I'll explain what I mean, below.

A company is sometimes referred to as an unnatural person. It is a legal conceit that divorces the activities and behaviours of the business from the people operating within it. The news people say, "IBM has laid off 200 workers," but IBM is a concept, it exists on paper. You can't touch it; it performs no actions. It is not real. The people working for IBM are real. You can touch them. They can send press releases, they can type memos, they can create reports, they can sell things, they can escort people out of the office holding a box of their personal possessions. A company is set up (arguably) to do one thing and one thing only: to maximise shareholder value. When someone has a singular focus and ignores all social mores and operates without regard for other people and without empathy, we refer to them as a psychopath[24] [25]. It's the same for a company. If you work for big corporations long enough, you will see the sort of behaviour that makes you scratch your head and

---

[24]https://www.psychologytoday.com/us/blog/our-humanity-naturally/201103/why-corporations-are-psychotic
[25]https://www.accaglobal.com/gb/en/member/member/accounting-business/2018/06/insights/corporations-psychopaths.html

wonder how the situation can occur. It defies logic. It makes no sense.

It's the same reaction that occurs when you encounter bizarre rules that come from your employer. Or they could be exhibited by an actual person that you work with.

And here is the issue: the newly minted analytics senior manager does not know how to deal with the psychopath, whether it is an individual or the company as a whole. They have made a career of being rational and logical. They have had stakeholders who have been aligned in their goals and methods. They can see how they fit in, and everyone is reasonable. Then, all of a sudden, they find themselves in a meeting and they think to themselves, "What the hell just happened? That person was totally unreasonable and was asking for all these things and making demands and it makes no sense."

And if that has happened to you, I'm sorry. It's not your fault, you're not going crazy, and I will outline some coping mechanisms and tips and tricks to prevent you being steam rolled.

Handle with Care

One thing you shouldn't do is to internalise their behaviours. It's incredibly dangerous to turn inwards and create an "us and them" situation. It's understandable though; you avoid the uncomfortable situation by minimising your exposure to them and run back to the comfort of the team. But this creates a toxic environment for the team and also poisons them against the non-analytics world.

Some ways that have been suggested to me regarding handling these people are (again, I take no responsibility for any outcomes from following any of this advice):

Go to Your Boss

It is a really good idea to bring the situation to the attention of your boss because they are likely to receive the complaints if the situation explodes. They can also give additional context to any likely motivators that you might not be aware of. It's important to have notes on the behaviours that you deem unreasonable so that you can show it is a pattern of behaviour, rather than an isolated instance or an example of them misspeaking.

Approach Them

This is a little dangerous if you don't feel equipped to have the sort of conversation that might ensue. Especially if you think that they are behaving unreasonably and there are no witnesses to what is said. But occasionally, professionally confronting someone who has been unreasonable is a good way of demonstrating that you don't want to embarrass them in public, but that you will hold them accountable. If they are simply someone who said something unwise – as opposed to being a psychopath – then they will recognise that what they did or said was unreasonable and you can have an adult conversation about the way forward. I've had this happen once and it's a relief when it occurs. But I think this is a rarity.

Approach Them (with a colleague)

If you are not the only person to feel that they are being unreasonable it can be incredibly comforting to bring someone else along for the discussion. It also gives you a witness to what is said in the room.

Go to Their Boss

If you are not able to get anywhere and you've talked to your own boss, you might have to escalate the situation by talking to the psychopath's boss. Again, you might gain additional context into where the behaviour is coming from and if you're really lucky you will find that they are aware of the behaviour and that they have a plan to deal with it. If you're unlucky, then there either won't be recognition that the behaviour is unwarranted, or they will defend the behaviour. If this occurs, then you are going to have to rely on your boss joining the fray. This is unfortunate because you are asking your boss to get into a fight that they may not have the stomach for.

Go Away, Write an Email

Sometimes it's difficult to respond to everything in the moment, and asking for the conversation to be conducted via email may give you the time and space to think clearly about the reasoning behind your decisions. The danger there is that the psychopath keeps coming back with counter arguments and counter points and so at some point it can be beneficial to end the conversation by inviting them to contact your boss if they want to take it further.

Support

If you're lucky as a brand-new senior manager, your boss may come to your meetings with stakeholders to then give you feedback. In these debriefs they can deconstruct what was said and how the other people in the meeting were trying to manoeuvre you into saying something or agreeing to take on a new piece of work. They can also give you advice on how to word your answers or how to lead the conversation away from dangerous areas and back to areas you're more comfortable with.

If they don't offer this and you're less confident than you want to be, you have a particularly problematic stakeholder, or suspect that a conversation may end up being uncomfortable, you should definitely ask them to come along.

Boss as Psychopath

But what if your boss is the one who is the psychopath?

A senior manager had risen to a very high position and their workload was prioritised in a committee consisting of their boss, who was the CEO, and the other C-sphere executives – four or five people in the room. They would go through the backlog and rearrange the workload according to trade-offs that they made – the marketing guy would agree to have this or that initiative pushed back if it meant that they could get something else down the line, that sort of thing. And then as soon as they walked out of the room the CEO would come to this senior manager and say, "Forget everything you were just told, these are the things I want you to work on next."

Now, what do you do? This is your boss, who will undertake your performance review and is responsible for your raise and your future prospects with the company. Additionally, they are responsible for allocating the company resources responsibly. They are also ignoring the agreed upon process to establish what that allocation should be. What are your options?

If you do what the CEO says, then you obviously have to manage relationships with the other stakeholders who are expecting their initiatives to be worked on. What do you say to them? What do you say to the CEO? If you expect the CEO to talk to the stakeholders and say that they have reprioritised their work, then you should expect to be disappointed because if they were willing to talk to them about it then they would have brought up their reasoning in the meeting.

So, you're looking at being caught in a squeeze between the stakeholders and the CEO. Guess what? That's an impossible situation. It's a lose/lose situation in which there is no good outcome for you. Start looking for a new job. If you tell your boss that you can't do what they ask, then you should expect to be replaced. If you do things their way, then the stakeholders are going to blame you. If the CEO was willing to be the bad guy for the other stakeholders then he would have, so you have to expect that they won't have your back.

So, what did happen to our senior manager? Well, they recognised it was an impossible situation and started looking for a new job. Surprisingly enough, the stakeholders also recognised what was happening without the senior manager having to talk to them directly and they acknowledged that they would have to manage the conversation. It was too late though, and the senior manager was let go before the stakeholders could hold the CEO to account for their behaviour.

The moral of the story? You can do everything right and still have an impossible situation. Keep your CV up to date, stay in contact with your network, and do not equate your sense of self-worth with your job. The less your job becomes about your technical skills, and more about who you are, the more fickle it becomes.

Politics

My interviews for this subject were undertaken with people who had managed to stay in senior management roles for some time, so the implication was that they were capable of playing the politics game reasonably well. That colours their responses somewhat.

Their advice coalesced around a few points: that politics was not necessarily negative, that not everyone was your enemy and that some people were actually trying to help. I could see why that might not quite ring true for people finding themselves in senior management roles for the first time. When you feel unprepared for the conversations that you are having and don't feel prepared for the sort of manoeuvring that occurs, it can be frustrating. Like every other aspect of analytics covered in this book, when you are unprepared or under-skilled in anything, then it's natural to be overwhelmed when you find yourself in situations in which that skill set is required.

Politically Aware

CLEVER   WISE

Game Playing   Acting with Integrity

INEPT   INNOCENT

Politically Unaware

Figure 8 Integrity vs Awareness

Furthermore, it's easy to be suspicious of people who play that game better than you. In the words of Baddeley & James[26], if you are a Sheep it's easy to think everyone else is a Fox. But, stress my interviewees, not everyone is out to get you! Politics is not all negative. Some people will actually be trying to help you. One of the more difficult tasks for the Propellerhead who finds themselves in a senior manager role is to figure out who to trust and how to navigate the environment. A good manager and a good mentor were important as a manager, but the senior manager without a strong political sense is even more dependent on that support network.

---

[26]https://www.academia.edu/47187961/Owl_Fox_Donkey_or_Sheep_Political_Skills_for_Managers

CHAPTER 15

Agency, Team Size & Culture

Agency

An unexpected side effect of interviewing the senior managers in preparation for this book was not that I had my thoughts and ideas challenged and augmented, but it was the amount that I learned about other industries and businesses. The people I spoke to were very candid about their challenges and some of the ways that they were addressing them, and I am very thankful for their time and openness. The learning I was most surprised by occurred when I was talking to a senior manager who had worked in an Agency business.

They explained that their goal when they worked with a client was to understand their business better than they did. No different than I have explained in the sections containing guidance for the IC and manager roles, right? But they then went further to explain the reason why. In Agency analytics, you can make money in two ways – one is providing the data to the client in such a way as to allow them to perform their own analytics on it. The other way is to look in detail at a business problem that the client has deemed worth spending money on investigating.

Great margins on the data provision, right? Set it up once, maybe there's a little troubleshooting or expansion periodically, but it's money for jam. And if you had to choose between a data job and an insight job, most people would go for the data job because the margins are so juicy.

But then the senior manager went on to explain why the insight job was more important. Fundamentally, the data jobs could be done by anyone with the required technical skills. They were commodity jobs. And as with any commodity, as soon as the client is approached by someone who is willing to do the same for less, the client moves to the new provider. Bye-bye, juicy margin job. That's the dangerous part of not having any barriers to entry.

So, the insights jobs are more important to lock into the business. When I was told that, I looked at him quizzically and said the obvious, "But surely insight jobs are just as commodified?"

"Sure, if all you are doing is answering the question that they gave you. Think of it this way. If you know the client's business better than them, and they come to you with a question, you can obviously give them the answer to the question, but you can then think of the, 'So, what next?' You can figure out the implications. And you can then give them the next thing that they need to think about."

"Can you give me an example?"

"Sure. An electricity company client of ours wanted some insight into the performance of a particular marketing campaign. We put together the results of that straight away and then we had a look at the results and took off our analytics hat to think about what the next question should be. In that case, the results of the question that they had asked weren't framed in terms of total profitability, merely in terms of sign ups and revenue brought in. To be fair, those were the metrics that the manager at the client was being judged by. And when we looked at profitability and churn figures for those new customers brought in, it really changed the perspective on the success of the campaign. And again, we thought in terms of our client, in this case the actual manager at the client who had brought us on. What question could we answer that would make them look their best? Because the campaign results would not move their personal needle in a positive direction. We figured out that we would have to come up with some recommendations on what to do next, otherwise the senior managers they would be presenting our results to would be left with the bad taste of the poor profitability figures. So, we came up with some historical analyses which supported a recommendation which would be a better approach than the original marketing campaign."

"That sounds all well and good but it looks like you were answering two questions that you weren't actually asked for in the first place."

He allowed that I was right. "Yes, but think about the emotions of the client during the presentation. You asked us to answer this question. We came up with this result. Happy client. But we thought about it and discovered that the initial question was misleading and because of x and y, so the result was actually bad. Now the client is thinking, urgh, how am I going to present this to my boss? My marketing campaign, which on the face of it worked a treat, was actually terrible. And then we swoop in and say, 'And because of x, y and z we think next time we should do *this* which should give us *these* results.' And all of sudden the rollercoaster ends on a high, because they have the ammunition that they need to go to their boss and say *this* is what we can do in the future. They have a way forward and can take the learnings as well."

"It still sounds like you have done more work than was required."

"True, but that recommendation is designed to require more insights when they implement it, so we get more work there. And the client has been given everything on a platter that they can present to their boss, so they know we're on their side, especially for warning them that the marketing campaign we were originally asked for, was not such a rosy picture. And so, we're demonstrating that we align our goals with theirs and that we know their business intimately, which means that we won't be replaced when someone comes along and tries to undercut us on price."

What I love about this story is that it is actually a metaphor for the IC chapter in this book. The technical skills can be replaced pretty easily. But the real business value is generated via in-depth business knowledge. When you are thinking about the work that your team is generating it can be handy to think about provocative questions like, "How will they use this? What is the next question that anyone looking at the dashboard will ask? How will this data change what they do? Can we get ahead of those questions? Can we illustrate this knowledge in a proactive way? How do we make our stakeholders look good in front of their boss?"

Team Size

I worked for Tripadvisor back when it was TripAdvisor. Steve Kaufer had previously run a software business, which had been successful until it wasn't, and Steve had presided over the expansion of the staff and then the cuts required as the business deteriorated. It was devastating to him and so his next start-up, TripAdvisor, was operated under the principle of extremely tight headcount controls. If a manager asked for an additional team of eight they might get approval for two. This was at a stage in the life cycle of the company in which we were on the up and making a lot of money. So, our Revenue per employee was very high. But most importantly the iron grip on headcount had two very interesting outcomes. First, it made the company incredibly focussed on what was important. There was no bandwidth for trying every idea someone had. So, we could only do a few things and we had to focus on delivering those things. This made sense and is not a criticism. Laser focus on the things that we believed would move the needle was a good discipline to have. The second outcome was that people's careers began to stagnate. We had very motivated, highly performing individuals who were not able to advance in their careers because their boss wasn't getting promoted because there were no other roles for them to get promoted into. That situation is sometimes referred to as Dead Man's Shoes.

I had also worked for two FMCG companies, Tesco over in the UK and then Countdown (part of Woolworths in Australia). The contrast between the resourcing of analytics in the UK and that in NZ was quite stark. We had something like 14 people doing all the work for NZ's largest supermarket chain, while at Tesco, admittedly a substantially larger operation, they had hundreds of analysts. Since then, the analytics headcount at Countdown has gone up to over eighty, so I think it's fair to say that we may have been understaffed while I was there. With the benefit of hindsight, I sometimes wonder what arguments I could have made to request additional resources.

Being a subsidiary of an Australian company, it might have been possible to refer to the level of analytical support in the head office or one of the other similar sized subsidiaries. I could have used metrics like analytical headcount per million dollars in revenue, or maybe even the analytics proportion of overall headcount. If I could have found the relevant industry metrics for the competition, that might have moved the needle. Some people have even hypothesised that there is a magic ratio of analytics staff to total staff. That strikes me as problematic, because of the different industries and employee bases for different firms. A supermarket chain has vast volumes of staff, which would lead to an immense analytics department should that magic ratio be adhered to. Likewise, an analytics consultancy would have a much higher ratio. One size never fits all.

Culture

I have heard that culture is the worst behaviour that the company will tolerate. I think that's a little bit of a jaundiced view on the subject. But it's interesting talking to people about the culture within their business and how that differentiates them from their competitors. It's natural to start discussions of culture on the pay and where the company fits with regard to how much it pays.

Pay

If a business is very small, then all the pay decisions will be at the will of the boss. If you find yourself in that situation you have my sympathies, because regardless of whether you are overpaid, under paid or paid about right, all the decisions will be made via emotion. Larger businesses have more time and more staff to consider their strategy around pay.

A story I consistently heard while talking to interviewees about applying for jobs post-covid was that there were four distinct experiences that caused the business to offer a particular salary range. Remember, post-covid an enormous number of jobs were advertised as hybrid, so all of a sudden, employers were able to tap into talent pools that were located further away from the office, and likewise candidates were able to apply for more jobs across the country.

The four strata seemed to be:

Regional businesses located in small towns. The salaries here were tiny because the cost of living was so much lower than in big cities. If you are just starting out in the industry, you might want to apply for these jobs as it will allow you to get a foot in the door.

Small businesses in major cities. The salaries here were higher, because the firms are competing with more businesses for the same resource, but the size of the business puts a ceiling on what they can offer.

Large businesses in major cities. It's possible to get manager level pay for IC level roles here. The size and profitability of the businesses enables them to offer large salaries.

And finally, businesses like FAANG (Facebook [before they became Meta], Amazon, Apple, Netflix and Google [before they became Alphabet], so would that make it MAANA now?)

On top of the size of the business and where they are located you also have considerations around where the business wants to be in the market. There is a huge cost implication in deciding to offer the upper end of the market pay scale. This comes into play when transferring between different offices of the same employer.

One person I know moved from a US office to one in the UK and wondered why their salary wasn't just converted from US dollars into UK pounds. They were informed that the pay scales for the different countries were determined by the relative cost of living. So, as the US office had a higher cost of living, the equivalent point on the salary scale for that job in the UK was lower. The person transferring was not happy!

These rules do offer the possibility of arbitrage. If a business has determined that a whole country has a particular cost of living and you, with the benefit of working from home, can find a low cost of living area to live in within that country, then you can take advantage of the higher salary range while keeping living expenses low.

Inventing Culture

You can't invent culture, but that doesn't stop people from trying. I worked at one place that was going through a problematic time and the senior management decided they would try to take some lessons from something written about how things were at Google. The study said that the best performing teams were those in which the team members trusted each other to deliver. The unwritten piece was that this trust occurred because the team members were good at their jobs. The senior managers did not look to address deficiencies in the performance of the team, but focussed on activities that would prove that the team trusted each other. This was regardless of whether the team members actually did trust each other to deliver their respective pieces of work.

Other workplaces come up with a buzzword or phrase that HR and PR have decided best represents the business, and they roll it out to great fanfare and then a month later it is forgotten. Regardless of how inspirational or motivational it was, whatever benefit they got from having a well-defined north star is lost because it was a one-off event. Compare that with Tripadvisor, whose motto was "Speed Wins," and it featured prominently. In fact, every time CEO Steve Kaufer spoke, he would preface his speech with a discussion of the motto and what it did and didn't mean. It was consistent and I think every member of the staff could probably recite his speech along with him, but it was important that everyone heard it and with acquisitions and what turnover there was, there were always people who hadn't heard it or needed a refresher. I also noticed that it was always engaging, no matter how often I had heard it.

One senior manager made the wry observation that the psychology of culture was sometimes lost on people who had come up through the ranks of analytics. The "propellerhead made good," so to speak. They mentioned that on one such occasion they had a morale issue in their department and the new senior manager who had come up through the ranks within analytics had looked puzzled at the latest results of the staff survey and made the comment, "I don't understand, we had staff drinks two months ago, why hasn't that fixed the scores?"

Secrecy

The culture of your employer can reflect the business assets that they hold and how they make money. I once worked for a business that had a single algorithm that they made all their money from. They had some very smart people who tweaked it and argued about it and did some very advanced mathematics with it, and, as you would imagine, they kept it under lock and key, the code residing in a stored procedure on their database server, kept on-prem because they didn't trust the cloud.

Now, I had worked for a start-up operating in the same space in a different country and so was naturally very curious as to how their algorithm operated – what factors they considered and how they approached the subject. I had already decided to leave the firm and had another job lined up and so thought I had nothing to lose to try to find out the code for this algorithm. Now, this was purely an exercise in intellectual curiosity, understand. While there was immense value in the algo and if I could get the code, I'm sure I could have taken it to any of the competitors and sold it for a sizeable sum, I had zero interest in doing so and to tell the truth that particular thought didn't even cross my mind.

The database that they were using was Microsoft SQL Server and I had been using that for a very long time, so I knew a few tricks. I needed them because the stored procedure that had all the code and logic in it was locked down very tightly indeed. I didn't have the correct membership to the groups that had access to the stored procedure, so I could not access it at all. Whoever had set up the security had done a good job. That's the standard way of stopping someone from accessing code that they shouldn't have, but they hadn't thought outside the box.

There is a system stored procedure that is installed by default in SQL Server called sp_helptext, which displays all the text about an object in the database. So, if you point it at a table it will tell you all the columns and keys on that table, if you point it at a function it shows you the definition of the function, and if you point it at a stored procedure it spits out all the code that was used to create that stored procedure. And it ignores the permissions of the person running it. It is a system stored procedure, so it runs as if it was the database owner and therefore has access to all the functions and stored procedures. Now, the bit the DBA arguably should have locked down was access to that sp_helptext stored procedure. But that's being a bit harsh on the DBAs, as they followed their instructions to, "Make sure only the right people have access to the stored procedure," which they did. What they didn't do was to make sure that there were no other systematic ways of accessing that stored procedure (and for all I know there may be others). And it's not an obvious vector for getting access to the code. So, no shade on the IT team.

While I was thrilled to have come up with a technical solution to my exploratory problem, I was a little disappointed at the actual code. Once I looked through it there was no magical pixie dust or even any advanced mathematical techniques.

Every employer tries to find the balance between too much security, which makes it hard for those who operate in the data space, and not enough security, which exposes the business to having external regulators imposing fines and regulatory scrutiny. I believe that it is impossible to get that balance perfect and so therefore the firm will tend to come down on one side or the other. And they usually come down on the side that means that they don't get fined or censured by their regulators. Therefore, you should expect frustration when you can't get access to the data that you need as quickly or as easily as you expect that you should be able to get it. It's important to learn what the firm's culture is regarding access of the data that you need so that you can be a responsible data citizen. This is also so you can learn the necessary steps that might be involved in getting access to new data in the future. You should also learn how long it might take to get permissions organised to access new data sources so that you can plan accordingly.

CHAPTER 16

Tips

Managing IC vs Managing Manager

It is more difficult managing people managers than ICs. ICs tend to be earlier in their careers and therefore less exposed to broken promises, bad managers and poor performance management processes. Managers, on the other hand, usually have metaphorical calluses brought on from being in the game for a little longer and having been exposed to more negative experiences. Hopefully some good experiences too, but let's face it, good managers are few and far between. Good employers are also few and far between. So therefore, managers tend to be a little more cynical, a little harder to motivate. On the other hand, they are more likely to give you enough time to prove yourself as they know the rhythm and the pace that the big companies operate at. They also do not have any of the presuppositions that naive ICs might have.

All Attrition Is Not Bad

When a firm has a single person who alone knows a tool or part of the business, we call this a single point of failure – there is the risk that if something happens to this person (by the way, never describe this in negative terms; don't say, "if this person should be hit by a bus," say, "if this person wins the lottery" – be careful how you phrase the loss) then the business will suffer an adverse impact. This sort of belief can become ingrained in the wider staff and can become part of the legend of the team, which may lead to the presence of that important person being integral to wider morale levels. Determining the actual level of a single point of failure is important (see the previous section on holding the firm to ransom), because from a structure point of view you need to know how important it is to cross-skill the team to be able to cover what they do. If you do have that person leave you need to know how important they really are and whether that warrants a counter offer. But frequently, when I spoke to senior managers about someone recognised as a key individual leaving, they all mentioned that it was a little bit of an anti-climax. I'm not sure how much of that was due to the correct level of handover carried out during their notice period, or if the legend of their importance was blown out of proportion.

The takeaway there is that not all attrition is bad – if there is a continuous departure of the team and continual poor employee survey results, then you could say that you may be in a death spiral. That is bad attrition: you are losing people who you would rather keep. If you find yourself in one of those situations, it is important to understand what's happening and how much or how little you have to do with it. If you know why people are leaving and you are not in the position to rectify the situation, you are in a hold or leave position: if you can stomach the situation then the option to stay and try to work on a solution is definitely on the table.

But let's talk about good attrition. It is possible (we saw it writ large over Covid), when people don't move on from jobs that aren't a good fit for them. Hiring is never exact and when a hire takes place in which the person is not a good fit for the job, it sometimes takes time for that person to realise that the role is not a good fit for their skills or temperament – or both. When there is a reasonable employment market, the person realises this and moves on by their own volition and finds something that is better for them. But when there is an impediment to that turnover of staff then you don't get that fresh blood, those fresh ideas or renewed vigour.

Hiding Progress

I was chatting with a CEO and asked them what their pet peeves were with analytics and they leaned back and said, "I hate it when I ask for the answer to a question and I don't get any progress reports and I find out that they've been polishing the answer or the dashboard or whatever it is, and that's very frustrating."

"Well, that's very understandable, right? You're the CEO and whoever is dealing with you wants to make the best possible impression. I admit that the analytics person should have asked you a really important question: is this something that you just need a rough answer, do you need something more accurate but non-repeatable or do you need something fully featured automatic and regular?

And the reason you ask these questions is that when I go into a new workplace and run my audit of all the workflows and dashboards, the ones requested by CEOs are the ones with the fewest views. This usually means that they've asked the question and the analytics people have created a dashboard, because that's how they answer a question."

The CEO nodded, "Yeah, they should have asked that because I definitely didn't need the full dashboard and automation."

I considered my next move carefully before continuing. "You know, if you're serious about avoiding the, 'Wait until it's perfect,' issue, you can do two things."

"What's that?" From his tone, I could tell I was taking a risk.

"When you ask for them to do something, ask them what steps they will take. If you want to know how long it will take then ask them to put dates on them as well. You're identifying the milestones and more importantly you're establishing how polished you need it to be."

"Ah, that makes sense. I can tell them, 'I don't need that' when they start talking about automation."

"True, but most importantly you are showing that you care about how it gets done. You care about the parts. And then you check in with them. I know you won't care when they say that they are exploring getting access to the blah blah data centre or that they are working with a different team on permissions and authentication. But what you're doing is showing that you want to know about the process, not just the end result. And you can always say, 'And so how far away from getting indicative results are we?' Because that again sets expectations of what we care about. And also shows that you may or may not care about the final gold plated perfectly formed result, just that you have an immediate need for indicative results that are allowed to be inexact or wrong as long as they are directionally right."

"True," he said as he nodded.

I didn't know if I had scored points by telling him that or if I had insulted him with something that he felt that he knew or should have known. You never know with the ego of a CEO.

Chaperone

It is frequently beneficial to take IC staff to meetings with clients or stakeholders when discussing requirements because they can understand the nuance of the task by being in the same room as the discussions. This can be especially helpful when you need to embed or access a client's systems in order to extract data for analysis, or alternatively pump data back into the client's infrastructure for them to consume it. It may be prudent to go over the ground rules of what they should say or add to the conversation, especially when it is a fee-generating relationship.

The story of one such situation was relayed to me by a senior manager who had brought his technical person to the meeting to meet the client's technical person, a "meeting of the quants," in their words. They were a bit surprised when the client's quant wasn't in the room when they arrived. The client was apologetic and said that, while eccentric, their quant was incredibly able and would be along presently. The senior manager relaying the story to me had nodded and kept an eye on their watch as the time ticked by. (I suspect they might have been playing up the outrage over being kept waiting because they would have been charging the client handsomely for their time). Eventually the technical person from the client's side came sweeping into the room, wearing a cape. They sat down with the manager's technical person and went straight into a highly technical jargon-laden discussion. I joked when he told me this and likened the impenetrability of the conversation to them spitting 1s and 0s at each other and the senior manager laughed and said it was like the old modems that you would connect to the internet with their screeching and boing da boing noises as they made a connection. Very technical and incomprehensible to both client and senior manager. After a bit of back and forth, the client's quant stood up and said that they were finished here and that they had somewhere else to be and after checking in with their own technical person, the senior manager thanked them for their time and the client's quant swooped out of the room. After they'd gone, the client smiled half apologetically and said that their quant was incredibly talented, if just a little eccentric. Sometimes you need both technical teams to be in a room to talk face to face without the managers getting in the way.

Promotions Are Needed for Team Growth

Ambition is interesting. In New Zealand the sign of a successful person is the three Bs: a boat, a bach and a BMW (a bach is a holiday home typically near or on a beach). Aspiring to global success is not typical there, as there are few examples of this as a role model. Where a particular person's horizon sits is not necessarily a function of where they were brought up. An individual's attitude to ambition differs widely, but the level of personal ambition has an effect on other people, as illustrated here.

A senior manager was telling me about their progression through their career and told me that their ambition was always just linked to whether they got a company car. If they were making enough and had the company car, then things were rosy. They didn't really have any ambitions beyond that and as a manager in their firm that was what they had achieved. They were leading a team, doing good work and were recognised for both their personal and their team's work. Happy days.

But then his team members started to bring this up in their regular meetings. They told him that unless he went for promotion to senior manager, their own careers would stall and they would have to leave the team to get ahead. When he went away and thought about it, he discovered that this was true. If he made it to senior manager, then he would have the opportunity to promote his senior ICs to manager positions and likewise his junior ICs to senior roles. He was acting as the bottle neck. And he owed his team those opportunities.

Data Democratisation

Analytics frequently supports business units who have a very high technical ability. Sometimes, that support consists of providing a stream of up-to-date, reliable, well-defined data that the business unit can use to self-serve the answers to questions they have, or power their own reporting or analyses.

On one hand this is great; the business can do their own thing without waiting for a ticket to be served in regard to accessing that data, there is a definition for every field that matches their understanding so they are dealing with data that is built for purpose, and typically it is enriched with other data sources (presumably, otherwise they would get their own data from the source system directly).

But humans are humans, and this can create a slight conflict.

From the analytics team's point of view, providing this data can be seen as chopping off the sexy half of the job. As you can see from the diagram of the six parts of the data analytics pyramid (figure 2), only two of those involve data wrangling. I've worked at a few places who have served semi-technical teams the data that they needed and one of the reservations from the team was, "It seems that we're being asked for only half the task here – shouldn't we be involved in totally replacing the work they're doing? We can replace that excel spreadsheet that uses the data or maybe make a dashboard that exposes the data point, which will drive action."

Part of the justification for the democratisation process is that it allows more people to utilise the data in order to do their job. While it is possible to replace those excel spreadsheets or to create a tool that creates the action plan based on changes to the data, the whole point is that there are other things that analytics can do, and providing the data allows analytics to act as a force multiplier.

So, how do you stop the team from feeling like data monkeys? Well, it's important for the team to understand that the provision of the data stops them from having to answer low level questions. That the range of uses for the data stops them from having to do boring work. But it is also important for the team not to feel like they are at the beck and call of the stakeholders. Batch changes so that they are managed like any other stream. It is probable that those members of the teams who consume the data will feel that they can come directly to the members responsible for the provision of the data to ask for a tweak or a change. It is important that they follow the process so that the team's autonomy is respected. At one place I worked, one of the team removed all the access permissions of the business unit using the data. When I asked them about it, they said, "They shouldn't have access to *my* data." I had to explain to them that there were two things wrong with that statement: it wasn't their data, and it wasn't up to them who had access to it. That particular situation was a symptom of a wider relationship issue that took a lot of time and effort to untangle and address appropriately. But I believe that their behaviour was driven primarily by the feeling of being a data monkey.

Fallacy: Data Driven Decision is the Apex

As a senior manager, you must clear your time and mind to be able to think strategically. You need to be able to consider the business problems and come up with solutions. Typically, organisations focus on being data-driven, and that has a certain element of truth to it – having enough data to be able to make decisions and having the culture of accepting data in the decision-making process are great things to have. But being data driven does not necessarily lead to the best outcomes. If the transportation industry 120-odd years ago was data-driven, then it would have been trying to optimise horses and carts, rather than considering how the automobile could change things. That's not throwing shade on them. It is only with the befit of hindsight that we enjoy the conceit of judging those in disrupted industries.

Think about it. You spend all your career thinking in terms of business problems and the data that you can get to try to solve these problems, but when it boils down to it, data is historical. It describes what has happened in the past. It is retrospective. It is not predictive. You could argue that advanced analytics – your machine learning and AI and what not – all have a swing at predicting what is in the future, but they're just pattern matching and while history has been known to rhyme, figuring out what is going to happen in the future is a lot harder than people think. Sure, lots of people will write a lot of articles and blog posts and make predictions because they are industry experts, and they want to make a name for themselves. But none of them have skin in the game. And the pinnacle of your career will be when you can take that time out and determine where the business needs to go, not based on where it's been and the data that describes it, but by looking beyond and linking what might be disparate data points.

Business Frequently Doesn't Know Data

One of the jobs of the senior manager is to be the PR person for the work that their team does. But making sure that the rest of the business knows about what the analytics team has delivered is only part of that PR role. A big part of the mind share component of the job is to not only preach what has been done, but also explain and illustrate the art of the possible – what kind of things that analytics can deliver. Why is this important? This is because it is not reasonable for the rest of the business to know the range of things that the analytics function can perform for them. Demonstrating some of the work that the team has completed will spark ideas about the sorts of things that they may want you to do, but is a good idea to have some proof-of-concept wireframes and research deliverables ready to go for the inevitable weeks that you don't have any specific recently delivered work. Don't be afraid to demonstrate the kinds of things that you and the team would like to do – even though technically that's a solution that is looking for a problem.

Having a strong relationship with the stakeholders is good because when you talk to them about their pain points you can make sure that you explore the wider range of those pain points, not just what they consider to be relevant to you – because if they don't know everything that you and your team can deliver, then they may not be giving you the opportunity to solve all their problems. They may only think of those that they think are relevant to their perception of your team's skills set.

And it's not their fault, right? They are in their position because of their skills and knowledge in their area, not due to their knowledge of what you do. Despite having been around for a while, analytics is still a nascent industry and senior management levels skew towards an older audience. So, while they may be very excited to use analytics, they may not have any experience with it and therefore may need assistance in terms of coming up with examples of how you might be able to help them.

Business Frequently Doesn't Know Business

It's always interesting asking stakeholders what single dashboard they would need to run their business. You would imagine that it is something that has already been asked for and delivered. And sometimes it is. But quite frequently I ask that question and get a pause and then a half shrug. I used to think this was a shortcoming of the stakeholders, but I've come to learn that this is not the case: let me explain.

When there is a single dashboard that can run a department or function, then this usually means that the nature of the business is very simple, and you can automate not only the reporting of it but also the whole running of that function.

But where the function is complex enough to have different approaches depending on the strategic direction of the business, the dashboards required to monitor the progress towards that direction have typically not been built yet.

What that means is that you need to be clued into what the objectives of the stakeholders you support are as soon as possible to find out where the unit is going and how you can best help them get there.

So, when the business doesn't seem to know what they want analytics to do, ask them if that's because they don't know this year's strategic objectives, or whether it's because they have not digested those objectives and turned them into their own tactical plans yet and therefore haven't figured out what to ask for from analytics. You certainly can't help with the first of those options but if it's the second option then it's a great time to start a conversation with the stakeholders so you can see how they are going to turn their business units' strategic direction into goals. Then, you can help shape their tasks for analytics to demonstrate their progress towards those goals.

Where to Now?

Where do you go after rising through the ranks to the top, or as close to the top as you want to go? As you rise, the number of roles available to you become smaller, and you need to be even clearer about where you want to go and what your driving forces are. The career question changes.

It may have looked like: let me manage more people. Let me manage more managers, support more parts of the firm. That's empire building, and may be desirable because salary and kudos are directly tied to the number of people in your function. But if you have five peers and the only job left in the firm within analytics is your boss's, then you might have to find other challenges that appeal.

This may make you frustrated. Especially if you're in consulting. There you have to come up with a sum of money to buy into the partnership. And the full equity partner path is becoming harder to achieve; whereas it was previously possible to make partner in your mid-thirties, now it's more likely to be forty.

So, it's important to know what excites you, so you can do that instead. As Peter the Recruiter says, "You've got to do what you love." And that can change. And sometimes it needs to change, based on what life is throwing at you. If you're going to have a family and want to be at home for that then having a role with travel obligations may be problematic.

Some of the options open to you include moving from Agency or Consulting to Industry to run a business line with fewer revenue obligations and more operational success metrics. One senior manager in consulting moved on from consulting and cashed in on their rolodex by running an incubator program with crowd sourced investors.

Another senior manager in consulting looked around after their last promotion, saw what they would need to do as a partner and that their firm was a little like a bunch of small business owners with very little support for each other – as long as they were making their own numbers then they were happy. Analytics wasn't really linked to a core offering and so what he could offer would never really be integral to any of the other partner's businesses. That didn't appeal and so when a head-hunter offered him a role in a new firm where analytics would be the core of the consulting proposition, he certainly liked the way that sounded. His new boss really sold him when he said that their goal was to get analytics into every business practise within the firm. That sort of partnership with other business units meant that they would always be front and centre in the business. A no brainer!

The beauty of working for a large multinational corporation is that there are frequently international opportunities for those senior managers who are looking for a new challenge. Being paid to flex your skills in a new environment or taking on a challenging project are other ways of keeping things fresh and seeing progress in your career. Plus, getting some time in a different country is great if you like travel for its own sake.

What Does Success Look Like?

The senior management role is interesting, and success for the other roles (IC and manager) is a little easier to measure. Senior managers are more routinely fired or laid off (than managers or IC) and this is because it is easier to ruffle feathers, to say the wrong thing, to be bad at handling fraught situations. But it's also more of a pressure cooker role with increased scrutiny, more opinions on performance, and most importantly, more people who don't understand your role having an opinion attached to it. I guess that's the flip side of the role requiring less technical focus and more personal skills: it's harder to objectively prove that you're doing well and therefore it makes your ability to manage messages, situations, and people much more important. That uncertainty comes hand in hand with the higher salary and increased remuneration at risk. This again makes your position vulnerable if the firm decides to look at cost cutting by letting people go. You save more by letting a senior manager go than you do by letting go two or three analysts. And who would do the work?

So, it's very possible to be a successful senior manager and still be fired. I'll pause there to let that sink in. A successful career at a firm can come to a point with an activity that you assume indicates failure, but it's nothing that you've delivered (or failed to deliver), it's not a people problem that you've handled incorrectly or any part of your performance that has caused this situation.

It could be that market conditions have deteriorated. Your department is no longer correctly sized for the market. The business has discovered that some of the work you do is duplicated by a department that is in a lower cost of living area, making the lower salaries there more attractive to the local talent, thus meaning that they can get the equivalent performance for less.

It's always possible to be laid off no matter what your performance is. That is why it is important that the business knows and appreciates the work that you do. It's important that you tell people. And the higher up in the organisation, the more wood behind your arrow there is. You are publicising all the work that all the people in your team are doing.

While it might be difficult to identify success, it's easy to see the failures and as Caroline Zimmerman[27] points out, analytics frequently operates as a canary in the coal mine.

> Over the years, I've noticed that data initiatives bring up all the dirty laundry in an organisation.
>
> If your processes are sub-optimal (and whose aren't?), it'll show up as data quality issues. If your organisation is siloed, it'll show up as disconnected data. If your organisation is very political, it'll show up as people not wanting to share data. If your organisation lacks strategic direction, it'll show up as a data strategy focused on fuzzy things that don't really have a clear value proposition.
>
> Data issues are just a proxy for broader organisational issues. Solving data problems requires a deep understanding of organisational complexity. And this is a big part of why I love it so much!

But what about success? We've talked a little about failure, or more importantly about how we shouldn't look at events as failures when they are just manifestations of the fickleness of the senior manager role. But success – what does that look like? In a lot of ways that's not up to me. You should have an idea of what success looks like to you by now, and whether your employer is able to help you achieve it. Some of the things that bring me joy:

- Members of my team growing into leadership roles, either internally or externally.
- More and more departments approaching analytics and requesting assistance.

---

[27]https://www.linkedin.com/posts/caroline-zimmerman-4a531640_over-the-years-ive-noticed-that-data-initiatives-activity-7011636145407074305-Nn7Q/

- Recognition at the C-sphere level for the successes that analytics enables.

Fundamentally, as you get higher up in the hierarchy, you will increasingly have to define what constitutes success. So, a more important question is... what does success look like for you?

PART 7

Unpopular Ideas

Controversy sells books. Disagreement, conflict and outrage all create attention in the media. This section of the book concerns itself with ideas that have a polarising effect on the people I share them with. I think they're all worth thinking about and discussing. My belief in them ranges from, "Hey, that's an interesting idea," all the way through to, "This is a hill I will die on." Please don't take any of them as personal attacks! And I'm fully aware that I have on occasion done the opposite of what I am recommending here. Sometimes you just have to be pragmatic.

CHAPTER 17

Unpopular Ideas: Part 1

It's Your Career

Historically, employees stayed much longer at their place of employment. My father worked at the same factory for thirty years, but nowadays people who have stayed at the same employer for five or ten years are considered "long-tenured." Previously, that loyalty was rewarded with career progression and a clear career path.

These days it can be difficult to identify a clear career path simply because they are no longer as common as they once were. Given that successful companies must often pivot to adapt to changes in the marketplace, and the half-life of many skills is now estimated to be five years or less, companies often have no idea what staffing needs they'll have in a few years' time or who would be qualified to fill them.

You can advocate for a career ladder. If your employer is too small then appreciate that the exposure to senior management, lack of bureaucracy and learning opportunity you have access to might have to make up for the less-than-concrete approach to advancement.

Frequently, HR will address a request for promotion with the statement that there are other opportunities if you move sideways instead of moving up. I used to hate this as an IC because I saw it as a sneaky move by HR – after (what I believed) to be me crushing my current role and being ready to move up, they wanted me to move to a different part of the business for a year (if on secondment) or for two to three years (for a transfer) until I learned that job as well. So, another two or three years of my service for the company at my current rank, with no guarantee that I would enjoy the new business unit or be as good at it as I was in the current role. I still have that attitude towards sideways moves, but I can see the point of them now. If you like your employer and are ready for a new challenge, and they do not have the promotion opportunity for you just yet (or they don't feel that you are ready for such a role), then maybe you need to do something else for a while, until there is that opportunity for you (or until you are ready for such a role). Instead of focussing on having to start from scratch to learn the new data, business unit, or relationships with the new stakeholders, you should see this as an opportunity to create more personal advocates.

But the point of this unpopular opinion is that you are responsible for your career. It's very important that you understand what I'm saying here. You are not responsible for how your employer treats you. You are not responsible for the opportunities that your employer gives you. You are not responsible for the market fit of the products or services that your employer offers, or of the market fit of the technical skills that you have.

But you are responsible for how you respond to how your employer treats you. You are responsible for whether you are ready for opportunities that pop up. You and only you are responsible for the decisions you make and how long you stay with your employer.

You Are (Probably) Being Impatient

I suspect most of the people reading this book are those early in their careers in analytics. As someone who is at the other end of their career, I am trying to distinguish between the characteristics of the (say) 23-year-old that were the same when I was starting my career and those that are specific about the current generation. If memory serves, there was a certain impatience amongst me and my peers when I started out – we wanted to obtain promotions and rise up the career ladder, and we were champing at the bit to be recognised for the awesome people that we were. I imagine that if you're just starting out, that is a frustration that you share. You have a lot to give but aren't getting the opportunity to express it. I hope that the tips given in this book help you with that.

Talking with people has helped me realise that this is the same impatience experienced by every generation. But is there anything at all that is different between me at 23 and today's 23-year-olds? What's the difference between generations?

Average tenure in roles is lowering. It's dangerous to try to come up with your own reasons for this occurrence, but one possibility is that people are less likely to accept being lied to (if they are – I'm not saying this happens at every employer) or are less likely to accept work environments where they are not able to achieve.

Perhaps tenures are shrinking because people have unrealistic expectations of what it takes to get ahead. Some of those expectations are set by the proliferation of information on the internet – not all of which is true. What it boils down to is this: companies won't give you promotions unless you prove yourself.

The opportunities to prove yourself are not guaranteed and come up sporadically. You can hunt them down or create them, but they still might not appear. Therefore, if you have a career path with set timelines you are probably going to be disappointed.

It's really hard to narrow this down to anything categorical because even though I have expanded my experience in this area by talking to a whole bunch of people in the business, that's still only 50ish sets in a world of experiences. One of the interesting things that has been suggested is that there is a stronger sense of entitlement nowadays. In contrast, twenty or thirty years ago there was an understanding that you had to work really hard to get those opportunities, but nowadays people are expecting the benefits of these opportunities as a given. One senior manager put it this way:

"People are saying that if they don't get a promotion, it means that this company doesn't care about them. And I feel like saying, 'This is a commercial relationship, and the company doesn't care about you. We care about the business value that you provide and in return for that we will give you the things we have put into the contract.' (I hasten to add that this person also meant that they will also treat the employee like a human being and wasn't reducing their treatment of employees to what was contractually obliged).

I suggested that surely twenty years ago their own manager would have had the same conversation with them. They sat for a minute contemplating that statement before shaking their head.

"No, back then I worked hard. I put in the hours. I was there on the weekends, I stayed late because the job needed it. I chose to put those hours into the work. But now the employees are expecting to be promoted even when they are working 9 to 5. They're not staying late. They're not going over and above."

So, I guess my unpopular opinion here is that any arbitrary career timeline will cause frustration.

How Long Should I Stay?

Twenty years ago, you shouldn't move before you'd served two and a half years, and the mode of tenure would have been close to three. Now it's not unusual for people to bounce out of jobs immediately if it is toxic or if they have a bad experience. Therefore, it is not as career limiting to explain short stints because it's acceptable to say that it wasn't a good fit or there was an issue. If you are going to bounce from a job for a whimsical reason, consider that if a recruitment agent was involved in you getting the job, they won't get paid unless you are there for a minimum period that is usually 3 months.

I personally was placed in a role that wasn't for me. I told my manager multiple times that I wasn't feeling it and then started telling the recruitment agent that placed me there the same. The feedback I got was consistent: just stick with it. The important thing to realise was that this wasn't a role that differed from what was advertised: this job was exactly as per the job advert. It just wasn't for me. It was more the way they did what they did that didn't fit with the way I thought. I didn't feel bad when I handed in my resignation letter because I had gone out of my way to communicate my unease to both my manager and the agent. The agent insisted on having a phone call to discuss my decision, but because I had talked multiple times with them about how I felt about the job, they couldn't really say anything. In fact, when I referred them to those conversations, they got off their high horse. The unsaid part of the conversation was that my peace of mind and good fit in a role was worth more to me than his missing commission. And more to the point, he had been given every opportunity to explore solutions that would have kept me there. "Just stick with it," was the sort of platitude that did not hold any water with me. The fact that I left maybe a week or two before the three months were up was what pissed the recruiter off. I did feel genuinely bad for my boss, though.

So, the unpopular opinion? Stay somewhere as long as you enjoy it. If you really don't enjoy the job, figure out why and put in an honest effort to help fix it. But don't stay anywhere just to avoid being seen as a job hopper.

Choose Opportunities Carefully

There were several Googlers among the people I interviewed for this book. One thing I made a point of asking them about was the 20% projects. Google wants you to innovate when you work for them, so they allow you to spend 20% of your time on projects that you self-select. Apparently, there is an internal site where you can select other people's ideas or post your own to get support. I always wondered if that was additional work or if it was really part of the normal work week. Or as I put it, "Are these 80+20% projects, or are they 100+20% projects? Are you working a 40-hour week with 8 being on this side project, or are you working a 48-hour week?"

One Googler allowed that some people did get excited and work hard on that side project and they warned that it was very important to select the correct project as your 20% project. As they put it, if you select something that doesn't really move the needle for the business, you could be working additional hours for very little reward. As a fictional example, at the end of the year your boss might be looking at your efforts to create a marketplace for used chewing gum and not really understanding how that was helpful for the larger company. Whereas someone who helped on the team that created Gmail might get more than just a pat on the back.

So, how do you make sure that what you are working on has value? Or how do you maximise the business value? This is one of the reasons that it is so important to have a good relationship with your boss. You need to have the benefit of their opinion. One of the worst things you can do is go off with your own opinion of what will generate business value and end up at the end of the year without the results you were looking for because you didn't want to validate your choices with your boss. That end of year conversation goes something like this:

"Hey boss, I think I deserve a promotion."

"Well, that's interesting, what kind of things have you done this year?"

"I did this project and this project and this project."

"That's great, well done. Those were good projects, and you did well in them. But that level of performance is what we expect from you here. What else have you done?"

"Well, I did this other thing."

"Oh… why did you do that?"

"I thought that would illustrate that I'm interested in building the work that we're bringing in."

"Ah. Did anyone ask you to do this?"

"No, I thought it up myself."

"I'm not so sure that this was a good idea. There is a whole department here who are doing this sort of work, and they have a set of operating parameters that keep an eye on things like brand values and concentrating on the clients and areas of work that we want to expand into. In fact, your efforts might have actively hurt their work."

"Oh."

My unpopular opinion here is that running with your own ideas is great, but a really good idea is to let someone you trust evaluate the business value of the idea you're approaching with such enthusiasm. That's sometime hard when you are in love with your idea.

Website

I think that you need a website. That's not an opinion shared by the decision makers at previous employers, but let me explain why it might be the case, as well as my reasoning behind the opinion.

Like most decisions, there is a cost benefit analysis. Senior management who don't come from a webtech background would overstate the difficulty of setting up a website while I, coming from a webtech background, naturally enough understate the issues with getting something set up. Now, let's look at why it is a good idea to set one up:

The first reason is the most trivial. It is cool to have your own vanity URL. Something like analytics.work.com if your company intranet was work.com. It's nice, it's clean and it's memorable. Whack a link from the intranet, make sure that the stylesheet and look and feel matches the corporate standards and you're away.

By controlling the user flow interacting with the various artefacts that analytics generates, you can shape the stakeholder behaviour. What I mean by this is that if you have some dashboards that should be looked at on a regular interval you can programmatically present the user the links to the dashboards that they have not seen at the required regularity.

From a functionalist point of view, you are free to use any technology that you desire, which means that you can use JavaScript to make user interactions more fun and intuitive. If you were simply looking to dump content at people, then Confluence, SharePoint and similar would be fine.

But being free to deliver whatever you would like works wonders when you are in a shared dashboarding environment; when you use d3.js for some visualisations and Tableau for others.

And you are totally able to link to all the dashboards from your menu system. Regardless of where the actual dashboard is served from, you can have a central menu system that serves as a one stop shop for your users. But wait, couldn't you make a menu page of Tableau dashboards from within Tableau? Sure, you could, but here is where the future proofing comes in.

If you are using Tableau On Prem, then it is always possible for IT to change the server addresses of the Tableau server. When that happens, if you are warned you in turn can warn your stakeholders. But if not, then you can expect a deluge of, "Where are my dashboards?" messages. And if you move from On Prem to Tableau in the cloud, then again you have those bookmarked URLs going to non-existent pages. Operating your own website allows you to isolate the users from what is going on behind the scenes.

But the juicy functionality you gain by operating your own webserver is realised when you have a portal that your users habitually use.

You can serve up personalised content based on your user's department and role. You can have a central point where all the users can be informed of data outages, delays or progress reports. On top of all that, you can align the catalogue of artefacts with the user base with the descriptions and documentation so that other team's onboarding can be improved. You can create walkthroughs, guides and introduce gamification to improve good behaviours.

The artefacts and tools made for analytics can be better surfaced from within such a portal.

I think I need to get better at demonstrating that it doesn't have to be a high-cost solution.

Max 4

If you have more than four direct reports or your manager has more than four, your career guidance is in jeopardy and your org has made the decision to prioritise operational effectiveness over your personal growth.

A lot has been written about optimal team size, and David Rutter has a nice summary[28]. While the optimum is four, David suggests a buffer is nice and recommends five to eight.

I would say that if I am managing eight people, then having an hour with each of the team (a level of engagement I consider an absolute minimum) would take up a whole day. If you lose another day to meetings and admin (which at the senior manager level is more like two or three days) then you have chewed up a lot of the week and now only have a day or two to do the rest of your job.

And I admit, four is arbitrary. I include it here because I see other managers who have ten or fifteen direct reports and the only thing I think is, "How can that org claim to have any support for that person's career?"

---

[28]https://www.artofteamwork.com/what-is-the-ideal-team-size/

Assessments

I have applied for jobs that have required coding or SQL assessments. I have stopped application processes because of the employer's SQL tests. I have also used these practical tests on candidates. My unpopular idea here is that you shouldn't apply for a job that requires a test. I'll explain why.

The first point is that the flavours of SQL have diverged significantly, which puts you at a disadvantage should the flavour you write differ from that of the marker. It gets worse if the person marking your work doesn't realise that there are different syntaxes of SQL and takes points off for using what they think is incorrect syntax.

Secondly, there are trade-offs in what you write that might not be appreciated by the marker. The same piece of code should be written differently depending on how the data is stored and whether it's less expensive to store the data or process the data. This makes deciding on whether to process large datasets in memory or through a series of temporary tables written to disk, a more pertinent decision. Related to this is whether the code should be written and optimised for execution or whether it should be written for clarity for the next person who has to come along and maintain it.

While it's less likely with analytics and SQL or coding tests, sometimes employers are less than ethical with the nature of the tasks that they use to test the candidates.

Especially in marketing. You don't have to look too hard before finding stories of candidates for marketing jobs submitting marketing plans as part of a test only to see their ideas replicated word for word in national advertising campaigns.

But the real reason not to do a SQL test is that the employer is usually looking for a particular answer. And it's usually connected with business knowledge of the data, or of the coding standards that they have. Either way, a brand-new person will not know the ins and outs of the data and which data points would be anomalous and which ones are ok. Or the analytics department's requirements for temporary tables over common table expressions.

CHAPTER 18

Unpopular Ideas: Part 2

The Curve Is Your Enemy

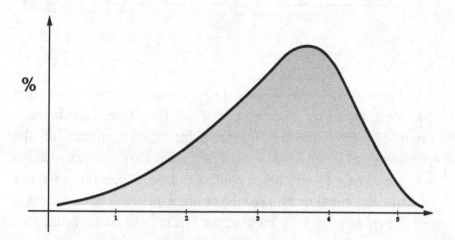

Figure 9 Performance grade of a high-performing team

This curve (fig 9) shows the performance of a team if the manager and the organisation are successful in setting goals for everyone, coaching and managing their staff's performance with honest and open conversations and those staff members have the skills and the motivation to perform at a high level.

The second curve (fig 10) shows the end result of calibration meetings to match an outcome that is dictated by the HR process.

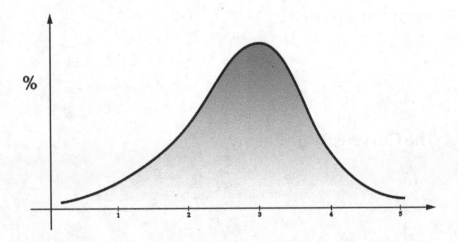

Figure 10 Rewarded Curve

If you grade on a curve, you are not reinforcing the behaviours that you want. I get why you might need to do this from a mechanistic point of view, but the fact remains: the aggregate of the performances you *want* is a totally different shape from the shape you are forcing the results to conform to. So, if you hire correctly and manage correctly and coach correctly then you have a skewed tail of performance with most of your team performing brilliantly. And if instead you reward performance on a forced curve, then you are reneging on the unwritten contract: if the employee does well, then they will be rewarded. I'll admit it: every place I've worked has done this, but that's because it suits the business. It flattens the funding needed for performance frameworks. What's the alternative? Fact-based calibration. *This* person did *these* things that means they were performing at a high level. If all people are performing at a high level, then the business moves in the right direction. And that's got to be worth the value of the bonuses.

I'll admit this is a naive idea because it ignores the difficulty in measuring the value to the business of the work that those in analytics do. In fact, I have a whole chapter on why that is impossible. And without that ability, how can you come close to aligning the value of the work of those in analytics with their reward?

But the fundamental issue is one that everyone has with the forced grading: it disconnects the reward from the effort. In fact, at one place I'm aware of, the manager keeps a badly performing person around just to balance the curve. What does that do to the team performance?

Story Time I

One tale that was relayed to me was from an analytics manager who lost a member of their team just before performance reviews. They were asked if they wanted a replacement from outside the firm or whether they wanted one of the internal candidates. The manager asked about the previous performance metrics of the internal candidates and then asked HR a few questions. Now, the team had originally had five staff, and they were all very successful and on the five-point scale where a one was, "About to be fired," and a five was, "Godlike." A five-member team was only allowed one two, three threes and a four. And most managers could not justify giving the lowest performing member of their team a 2 so a lot of teams ended up getting a 3 for everybody. But being a good manager, he really wanted to give all his remaining team fives, because they were performing that well. Of course, HR would say no.

If he brought in a new recruit from outside the firm, they would get a two and he would have one four and three threes to give to a team who should be getting fives. So, he thought outside the square.

While going through the performance history of the internal candidates he discovered there was someone there who was on their way out. They had a history of bad performance and weren't a good fit for the firm or the roles that they were attempting. So, the manager took this person into their team. Why? So that they could change the shape of the curve. They could give that person a one, which meant that the manager would have a five to give to one person in the team. Or they could give two fours. So, without having to go to HR, the manager could give the new person a one, and two of their team could get fours. The other two would have to get threes. And then the manager went to HR and told them how well the team were performing, and could they get dispensation for the two threes to be bumped up to fours? HR came back and said that one of the threes could be a four. So, while the manager was still fuming that his highly performing team couldn't all be recognised because of the curve, they at least had some recognition for their good work.

I commended the manager on their thinking but asked if they were worried that their three would leave because they were now the only one of the high performers who wasn't getting a four. The manager smiled and said that they had a bunch of extra opportunities and non-financial rewards (training, presenting opportunities, that sort of thing) that were tailor made for their specific circumstances, so they were able to support them in other ways while maintaining their morale.

In summary, the scores for the team went from

3 3 3 3 3 = 15

   or

2 3 3 3 4 = 15

to

1 3 3 3 5 = 15

1 3 3 4 4 = 15

1 3 4* 4 4 = 16*

*HR approval required

Story Time II

I frowned as I spoke to the manager from the first story and said, "But now you have to manage a non-performer out of the business, that's a lot of stress and hassle," (this was in a European country where letting go an underperforming member of staff has a legally mandated process that can take a number of months).

The manager literally laughed. "I thought so too, but something weird happened. We had a software project from a separate team that was going poorly. The Engineer on the project was... eccentric. They didn't comply with coding standards and there wasn't enough oversight on the project until late in the piece, so nobody knew he was naming his variables things like a, b, c – instead of variable names that showed what the thing was like DateOfPurchase or NumberOfItems." They could see my mouth open to start a discussion on which naming convention to use

(Camel case starts out lowercase with each word starting with a capital letter, like dateOfPurchase or numberOfItems. Pascal case is similar to camel case, but the first letter is always capitalised, like DateOfPurchase or NumberOfItems. Snake case means that we delimit words with an underscore like date_of_purchase or number_of_items) and so hurried to continue the story. Now, this project was a big deal for this other team and the manager only discovered how badly things were going late in the piece. So, the analytics manager was told by their boss that they needed to help: one of their team would need to be seconded. Send them your best person, he was told. "So, I sent them the person who had gotten a one. Stuff them, I wasn't putting my own projects at risk."

"Ooh," I said, wincing. "How did that work out?"

They looked at me with disbelief. "It went really well. Our guy somehow was able to get onto the eccentric coder's wavelength, was able to get into their head and persuade them to make their code readable to other people and to simplify it. The process of the eccentric fellow explaining it to our guy meant that they effectively refactored it while they were explaining it and so it performed better as a result of it matching the coding standards. And so, the project was a success and they ended up winning company awards and getting one-off bonuses for it."

"So, you accidentally found the perfect job for the underperformer and didn't have to fire them?"

"Exactly! And because they were on the project for so long, I could do the same trick with HR to get the rest of the team their better grades (I rotated who got the three and made sure the new three got a lot of other benefits) and then after that performance cycle, the manager of the eccentric coder wanted to make the secondment permanent."

"Lucky!"

So why is this an unpopular opinion? It's because the current "forced curve" does have its benefits. It restricts the amounts paid out to staff so it's beneficial to the bottom line. It's an easier process from an HR point of view. Simple rules and processes mean that HR and people managers don't get bogged down in the details.

Ebb and Flow

I have a joke that every five years senior management will have a crisis of faith in analytics and call in one of the Big 4 or one of the Global Consulting firms and ask them this question: should our analytics teams sit with the business unit that they support, or should we create a Centre of Excellence where all the analysts sit together? The confusion comes from whether they want to maximise the ability of the analyst teams to learn the business and maximise the business value that they create by being closer to their stakeholders, or whether they want to maximise the technical abilities by having the analysts maximise their exposure to other analysts.

If the firm currently has a decentralised analytics function, then the experts will stroke their chins and after a month or two hand over a bill with five or six zeros on it and say, "You should Centralise." If the firm is centralised then they will stroke their chin and after a month or two they'll hand over a bill with five or six zeros on it and say, "You should Decentralise." And in five years' time they'll come in and do it all over again.

Do I think that's right? Well, with working from home being so prevalent it almost doesn't matter. Nobody sits with anyone anymore. If I had to be in the office two days a week, I would try to spend one day with my stakeholders and the other day with my technical team or peers. And that would be the same at any career level. The one thing I would like to call out is that if you are in a Centralised team with all the technical people together, then this can counter-intuitively lead to the reduction of the analytics role to just the technical parts. So, you become a data monkey or a reporting monkey: you become a human cog in the machine of generating the artefacts, rather than providing the deep insights that really move the needle for your stakeholders. While this will increase your team's technical capability, I've just spent a good chunk of this book explaining how the deep knowledge of the business is where real value is unlocked. What you are doing is making your team more employable elsewhere instead of maximising their ability to generate business value in their current role.

There are actually two unpopular ideas there: the first is that the Centralise/Decentralise investigation is a waste of time and money (certainly unpopular with the consultants charging for the investigation!), and the other is that any team that concentrates on the mechanics of preparing analytics artefacts at the expense of learning about the Business dehumanises the employees working there.

Quo Vadis?

It's Latin for, "Who goes there?"

It's very important with IT systems to know who does what. One of the reasons IT have rules against sharing passwords is so that if, say, an obscene email is sent, then there should only be one person who could have sent it. It's so that you can hold people accountable for their actions. It's the reason that servers have access logs and why we have complex rules around acceptable passwords and processes around user account management.

An issue with analytics is that some of the tools that we use require them to run using what's called a service account. This is an account that might not have a password that can be used by server level programs, and therefore has heightened permissions to move files around or access certain databases for example. The kind of things you would need if you were running ETL processes.

But these two desires, the demand to know who has done what, and the ability to run automated ETL processes, are not commonly compatible.

It is possible to have systems in place to gain that ability, but let me explain what can happen if you do so.

Let's say you have an automated process to move data from a source system into the database that you use to generate your reports. There is some light enriching of the data using some other databases and maybe some staff data in there as well. It uses a server account because its best practise not to allow a personal login to access the database and because the source database is also locked down except for "machine to machine" connections.

Now, let's say that your reports are very important. Let's say that they are used by the CEO to make strategic decisions. Or for the legal team to keep the regulators at bay. Now, let's say that someone in analytics makes a change to the ETL that incorrectly calculates a metric that is central to the dashboards.

And now you're asked to find out who made the change and what it should have been.

Most of the places I've worked have not had the necessary systems in place to answer that question. Anyone who has access to the tools that analytics has can make the changes and there is no way of detecting who did it.

How do you protect against this?

You borrow some of the tools from software development. This is where the unpopular opinion comes in. You need to control who has access to making changes to the code that you are running. So, you lock down who and how code goes live using the tools that you want to use, usually by implementing some form of code repository like Git. This is effectively a database of all the changes made to a code base. In this case, the code that does the ETL. Then you make sure that the only way that code can go live is by being pushed from the repository. This ensures that there is a person who is held responsible for every code change and the code can still run under the server account and still has all the access and permissions required.

Why is this an unpopular idea? In small and immature analytics orgs, anything that gets in the way of delivering the result is seen as unnecessary red tape. While I would hope it would be clear that this level of holding individuals responsible for what they do is desirable, there is frequently resistance in implementing these governance steps.

You Can't Estimate

The proximity of analytics to Software Engineering has led to the adoption of SWE frameworks to manage work in analytics. Agile has been the most prominent of these and whenever a person says, "We use Agile here," I always smile and ask what that means in reality. Nobody has a pure implementation of Agile and so the interesting thing for me is which bits are adopted. And it's more helpful to get someone to itemise them rather than assuming anything. It usually means something like, "We have daily stand-ups, monthly retrospectives and use story points to estimate durations of tasks."

Story points are an attempt to increase accuracy of estimation by making the metric fuzzier. They usually use some version of the Fibonacci sequence and are an attempt to distance the estimation of how long something will take from the measurement of that duration in units of time. So instead, they use story points that are defined in terms of units of time. I don't quite understand that leap in logic. Sometimes those story points are changed depending on who is doing the work. Nothing says that you are a valued member of the team like saying that a task will take 4 story points if someone else does it or 6 story points if you do it. One day you'll be able to do it in 4 story points. Maybe. And then if you don't deliver it in the time equivalent of those story points, what happens then? Are you expected to work weekends and long days to make sure you hit the arbitrary deadline based on the story points that aren't time units – but are, really?

I think that story points are dishonest. I think they are there to try to remove the implied exactness of estimating tasks. If you say something is "small" then you're right whether you think it should take 3 hours or 4 hours or 5 hours. But if you try to estimate something as taking 3 hours then you can be very wrong if it takes 5 hours. Estimation is fundamentally wrong because you are trying to get a single number to represent the time a task will take for planning purposes.

Brad Yarbro wrote that one of the hardest things to do as a data scientist is estimate time for a task.

> *Hofstadter's Law: It always takes longer than you expect, even when you take into account Hofstadter's Law. I try to give myself extra time to account for the unknown or other requests popping up. But even trying to account for the unknown, I still underestimate the time it will take on occasion. Hofstadter's Law is funny because it feels like you should be able to account for it, but according to the law, you can't.*

So, if t-shirt sizing is no good, story points are no good and estimating hours or days is no good, what would you suggest?

How about giving a distribution of *likely* completion times?

Be sure to get in writing that you are presenting each *component's* most likely completion time and that you insist that the stakeholder acknowledge that each task has a non-zero chance of taking a much long time to complete.

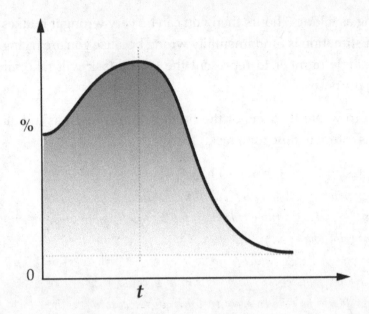

Figure 11 Probability of a particular task taking a particular time.

And then, with the cumulative likelihood you can say that while the most likely time for the whole thing to be completed is x, that there is a non-zero chance that it might take as long as y or even longer – that tail keeps going!

The important part here is that the most likely completion date will be *t*, but that there is a chance that any of the three sub-tasks takes longer than expected and therefore pushes out the actual delivery date accordingly.

The point here is that you are demonstrating that it is an inexact science in estimation, and you are demonstrating the scale of how long it might take. And more importantly that there is a non-zero chance that the total time might be very long indeed.

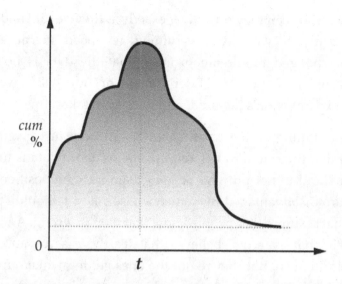

Figure 12 Cumulative probability of a number of tasks being completed in a certain time.

It's also great to go into meetings with a list of your assumptions or uncertainties. My favourites are the conversations regarding data.

"You've got here where the data steps are likely to take a week and could take a month, but IT is telling us that the data is automatically populated in this table, and they've provided a description of the fields and everything."

"Yes, I know. And as you can see on the distribution there is a line right here that represents a single day. So, if what they're saying is true, then we can tick that box and move on. "

"So why does the distribution go to a week and then beyond?"

"Because (and no disrespect to our IT team) the situation with data is never as senior management tells us it is. Until my team has gone in and kicked the tires and had the data flows running without incident to the agreed SLA and have signed off on the data hitting our environment in the correct format at the right time and without issue, then I'm sorry, I'm going to treat the claims as political promises. I guess I have been burned by promises and assurances once too often. And so, if they do deliver exactly as they've said and more importantly if we have everything we need (because undefined or changed requirements mean that the data is not sufficient, through no fault of the IT department, of course) then we may need to expand what's ingested, and that again takes time."

What you're outlining is that trust is earned, and not just given blindly. And that the standard response to claims about data is to smile and nod and to not put you or your team into the position where they are disadvantaged by someone else's lies. I shouldn't say "lies" – that assumes that people know that they're wrong. And it's very likely that everyone believes that it's the case because everyone tells them so. But they're not the ones getting woken up at 6am because the dashboard is wrong because an element does not perform as per specification.

So, why do people insist on estimations? It's because when you're managing resources you attempt to play Tetris with the two dimensions: the business value that you can unlock and the human resources that it takes to unlock it. The theory there is that you can make trade-offs to unlock business value quicker by deciding to work on one project instead of another. Basically, you can have x amount of value from each of three projects that are about 2 (whatever 2 is) and the theory is that the manager can compare that with y value that would be unlocked by completing two lots of a 3 (whatever a 3 is). And only a manager can make the complex calculus that compares x with y.

One manager explained to me that the reason that they do this is to slip into the sprint planning of smaller tasks that would release additional business value earlier than otherwise planned. The argument there was that it was better to delay the big job that would realise a large amount of business value in a matter of weeks so that you could deliver the smaller amount of business value from the smaller task, earlier. An IT manager at the same firm explained to me that the flavour of Agile they use rejected that idea because the business stakeholder who had groomed their backlog had categorically decided that they would be willing to delay the small amount of business value that would be delivered by the smaller tasks in order to focus on getting the larger business value project delivered without delays, even if it took a lot longer.

It's almost a religious argument – everyone has an opinion and there are so many variables that a scientific examination of what is the best approach is always going to be problematic. This is why it's in this section of the book.

How Long?

I flat out refuse to let a stakeholder decide how long something will take. The more technical they are, the more difficult this becomes. The more important the stakeholder is, the more careful I must be in having the conversation. But as soon as the stakeholder starts presenting an opinion on how long something should take, the closer they come to trying to manage your team. Obviously, that is a dangerous place to be!

Why is that so problematic? For a start, it presupposes a level of technical knowledge of the data and dashboarding that is unlikely to be backed up by actual facts. As with any other situation where opinion does not match actual skill, it is dangerous to rely on their estimations. They also ignore the possibility of unknown confounding situations popping up. The less the stakeholder knows, the more likely they are to be certain of their opinion.

So, how do I dissuade the stakeholder from having an opinion on how long something should take? A big element of why they come up with an opinion is to fill the void – the uncertainty of how long the task will take. They may need to know the duration of the task for their own planning. And if it won't be provided, then they will make it up. The biggest error you can make is to agree to their estimation. Actually, the biggest error you can make is making a half-hearted attempt to have an agreeable discussion and have a vague, non-confrontational refusal to agree to their estimate. That makes you both leave the meeting thinking different things: the stakeholder thinks that you are on board with their estimation while you think that you have stopped them from thinking that they know the deadline.

So, you have to make sure that this doesn't happen. One way is to halt the conversation, make sure that you have their full and undivided attention and say, "I'm not sure that you're hearing me. I don't think that duration is right. I can't tell you how long it will take but I can tell you it won't be that long. It's much more likely to take longer. Can you tell me why you need a deadline for this piece of work?"

Focus on the reason they need a deadline. Because if you agree, or even if you just fail to say no, you are swapping their operational need for a deadline to a commitment from analytics, and then that flows through to a requirement for your team to work late and weekends to get the work done on time.

One of the most dangerous phrases I have used is, "You think it could be done in a week? I think you're right, but the environment would have to be exactly as you've described, there would have to be no issues with access or permissions, we would have to have no other work to do and there would have to be no interruptions or any of our regular meetings. I don't believe any of that is likely to be true, so why don't you tell me why you are so keen for this to be delivered so early and we can see how we can help you manage your stakeholders' expectations."

Oh, and by the way, the sideways request, "Can you just pull this data for me quickly?" should be protected against. That's when someone comes up to your data engineer and "just" wants this or that data pulled. Because it's obviously a tiny job. This sort of thing saps the data engineer's will to live because it diminishes the work that they do, it dictates how long it should take, which ignores the complexity of what they do, and it assumes that whatever that data is it will be worth more to the business than whatever else the engineer has got going on. This means that the work that they would be doing instead is not worth as much as what the stakeholder has decided that they should do.

This is an unpopular opinion because it has the potential to mess with the relationship between analytics and their stakeholders. But if you get it right, you and your team will have a better work life and more respect for your time and the work you do.

CHAPTER 19

Unpopular Ideas: Part 3

Problems with Data

A call centre I worked at had an enormous issue with the accuracy of data. Actually, they didn't, but they had done historically, and the impression of inaccuracy remained even after they went to great lengths to address the issue. The call centre housed outbound sales reps who were paid based on their success in converting leads into sales. A hugely complex set of rules governed which successes counted towards their bonus calculation. Originally these rules weren't 100% implemented into the ETL process, and so there were a few anomalies and exceptions with edge cases. By the time I came along the previous manager had dedicated one of the team to be the subject matter expert and they spent most of their time making sure that the ETL process reflected the rules that the sales reps had been told about. But the damage had been done.

There was the perception that the data was fallible. And that it might be worth complaining about the data because the worst-case scenario was that they were right, and some data should be counted when it wasn't currently being counted and therefore, they should in fact have a higher bonus.

As part of the research for this book, I've asked senior managers what they would do in this situation to regenerate trust in the data. I received an answer that I wasn't happy with: that I should get rid of the entire team that was responsible for the ETL process and replace them with new people. The theory is that only by scorching the earth can you start fresh and get that trust in the data back.

What did we do instead of that? Well, it seemed that the published rules weren't being mapped to the data that we were presenting, so we created a flow chart that reflected the logic that we were using in the ETL so that the sales reps could check themselves that what they suspected was an incorrectly missing sale was actually correctly missing. But that didn't reduce the number of data complaints that we were receiving. They weren't using the documentation or our flowchart. So, we added a checkbox on the data complaint form to say that the sales rep had in fact checked the flow chart. No change to the volume of complaints, just a bunch of checkboxes checked without the corresponding activity of actually checking the flowchart. Frustrating. But again, from the point of view of the sales reps, understandable. It cost them nothing to submit the complaint and they might get a higher bonus, so nothing ventured, nothing gained, right?

We started to deliver a view not of the sales and leads that were within the rules and should therefore drive the sales rep's bonus, but *all* the leads and *all* the sales, along with a note about whether it counted towards bonuses or not – and most importantly, the reason why. The thinking there was that we were pre-emptively telling all the sales reps why the data was or was not included. So, they wouldn't have to raise a data complaint, all the answers would be there, available to them.

But that wasn't going to solve the problem. The problem was one of trust. And like all matters of trust, you don't just receive it. It takes time. You have to earn it.

So why is this chapter in the section about Unpopular Opinions? Because I want to talk about the way I should have handled this situation. And this will be unpopular to some.

As discussed, the issue is one of trust. And trust is eaten away by every person who doubts the data in public. And the way to regain that trust is to take an aggressive stance on every challenge. And by that I don't mean aggressively reacting to the reporting of a data complaint! No, that implies that you are sensitive to the data potentially being wrong, when the opposite is in fact the case. We are confident in the data being right. And what you want to do is make it very public and aggressively demonstrate that you are doing the right thing. My solution to regaining the trust in the data is twofold (and again this approach has a lot going against it, so think twice before trying it yourself).

First of all, make every challenge to the data very, very public. Make sure you name the person who raised that challenge, and deliver your findings very publicly. "Donald in the Broadband team raised a query regarding their sale on Tuesday. Donald was right to do this because if Tuesday's sale was counted, they would have received an extra $150 in commission, so we investigated it straight away. It turns out the sale didn't count because the opportunity was raised under a purchase order by Corporate. Donald would have seen this if he had checked the flowchart that is updated and still available on the intranet at this address."

By making everyone who raises a data complaint accountable for the time it takes to investigate each complaint, hopefully we would have reduced the volume of complaints. And we would have had to own all the actual errors, but by this time there were none. Every single data complaint was an unreasonable slur on the team's good work and added to the distrust of the data. Naming and shaming would not have been a smart move in reality.

My second unpopular idea, which I also did not implement, was to increase accountability of the sales reps who made the data complaints. As I mentioned, there were no negative consequences to raising data complaints. So, the idea is that I stand up (either figuratively because we're on Zoom or literally because I go to their office) in front of the salesperson team and I say, "Hey folks, we know that the data used to be bad, but we've worked really, really hard to get it right and we've been successful in doing so. So much so that I stand behind every single data point. So, I invite you to lodge all your queries about the data because I will pay everyone in the sales org €10 if it turns out that you're right and the data is wrong. There's what, a hundred sales reps in the team, yeah? So, I will be personally out of pocket €1000 if any of our data is wrong. Sounds pretty good right? €10: that's one day's lunch or a cocktail the next time you're out at night. Plus, on top of that it might mean that you get more commission, if that data point is enough to bump you up to the next level. Nice. But," and here I would raise a finger and pause, "if the data is right and you are wrong, I want you each to reach into your pockets and pay me €10. Everyone in the team. Now, I'll remind you that all the rules for the commissions are published on the intranet and we've even built a nice little flow chart to show what is considered and why an opportunity would fall out of consideration, so there should be no surprises. But I want you to be pretty sure of yourself if you think that the data is wrong."

Now this wouldn't work in reality: the data involved is personal so you couldn't expect their peers to check that the data query was legitimate before submission (although why their team leader couldn't check the data query, I'm not sure) and it's a terrible move to try and punish the whole org for the actions of one person and doubly so when you're trying to take money from the team. So, maybe the reason I didn't do this is not because I lacked the cojones, but more because it's just wrong to do it – but at least it illustrates how hard it is to regain trust when it is lost.

The Office is Necessary. Sometimes. Maybe

I hate the daily commute. Always have. I used to walk half an hour to catch a bus for an hour at 4am to get to a factory job. If you missed it there was an hour wait until the next one. I used to travel two hours each way each day to get across London on two trains, a bus and a shuttle bus, and you can imagine the delays if you missed a connection by a minute somewhere along the line. So, rest assured that the whole work from home thing was incredibly attractive to me, even if the reason it became widespread was tragic.

However, I think there is something to be said for spending time in the office with your colleagues. I do not say this because I have a huge commercial property portfolio. I just think there are some benefits, and some circumstances that can't be replicated by working from home.

White board sessions where ideas are debated and the reasoning behind the value decisions are given is a really good way of illustrating the way of thinking that junior members of staff should be modelling from those seniors. And this is one of the only ways to get that value judgement communicated to the team so that people can learn from it.

A lot of people share my appreciation of the benefits that work from home brings, and they react quite strongly to any attempts to remove or reduce the number of days that they enjoy working from home. I expect a reaction to this idea. And just to be clear, I'm not saying everybody should be in the office or that we should all be in the office all the time. Just that there is an opportunity for juniors to learn from seniors and this method is only available in person.

You Can't Share

Sometimes you get news that you can't share. I had given my letter of resignation and was working out my notice period (one month and contractually required). One of our vendors rang up and told me that they were very sorry to hear that I was leaving. At that point I thought they were being polite. Very nice, say some empty words and hope we bump into each other at a different firm. But they continued. They said that they were sorry I was leaving because whenever they dealt with me, they could feel that I was only working with genuine intent to solve the problems and that I did not have any ulterior motives and because of that I was going to be missed. I looked around the open plan office and realised that this was the sort of call I wanted to have on speaker phone. Lovely feedback from an external party praising my behaviour in a business relationship. I wanted everyone to know so I could take full credit for it, but it wasn't the sort of thing you could really share with anyone or even ask for them to write in a reference because it was so self-serving and self-congratulatory. So, I had to write a book to get the story out there (lol).

The point here is that hopefully during your career you will be blessed with similar vignettes and stories that you can't share – they will only be for you. Some of these will be feedback from staff you have managed, either while you are managing them or after one or other of you have left your employer, when they will say how much the time that you spent with them meant. It means a lot more after the fact when there is no career benefit to them for saying such things.

The Latest Thing

Adam Sroka[29] said:

> *Businesses these last few years:*
>
> *- We need to do blockchain*
>
> *- No, wait, now we need to do low-code AI*
>
> *- No, wait, now we need to do data mesh*
>
> *- No, wait, now we need to do LLMs*
>
> *If you keep chasing the next big thing, you'll get nowhere.*
>
> *Ask yourself: Are these in line with the strategy or shiny distractions?*
>
> *Stay disciplined and critical, only then will being open-minded and innovative pay dividends.*
>
> *And you're looking around at the mess of the data and say to yourself that we can't even get clean data on time and people are talking about AI? Let's focus on getting the basics right first, hmmm?*

A very wise man said it was important to know when to get on or off the hype train. I thought that all hype was BS, but he quite rightly corrected me and said that it's fine to invest enough to warrant the additional investment that might come your way for ticking that box. In their case it was to have enough time and resource invested in bitcoin, blockchain and AI without putting all their eggs in those baskets, because their investors wanted to play

---

[29]https://newsletter.adamsroka.co.uk/p/shiny-object-syndrome

in those spaces and there was benefit to that. But they weren't fanboys. They knew what they were getting into.

It's a sample of one so I don't know if this is an approach for everyone, but that level of sophisticated thought came from someone who wasn't a technical person – and so therefore they didn't have a vested interest in investing in that tech just so that they could play with it – they could afford to see the tech for what it was and how much or little that they should invest in it so that they could get the value from it. A pretty good lesson there!

So, I guess my unpopular opinion is either,

> *It's ok to be involved in the flavour of the month technical darling buzzword as long as you size your exposure to it correctly.*

Or,

> *Ignore the flavour of the month technical darling buzzword and just focus on delivering business value.*

It depends on who I am talking to.

Speaking of AI

AI is the big buzzword of the moment and there is great interest in locking in the promise of greater insights with fewer team members. Naturally enough I brought this topic up with my interviewees, and I got a range of responses, two of which I want to highlight here.

The first relates to why it will be difficult to unlock the power of AI and Machine Learning. As Chad Sanderson says on LinkedIn:

> *Some people believe that AI will automate the work of data analysts.*
>
> *That might be true. However, it's only going to happen when the work of data analysts doesn't involve figuring out which data to use, where the data is located, where it's coming from, why the same column is present in 4 different databases each with different numbers, what it means semantically, how it's changed over time, wading through all the gotchas and layers of filters in SQL, going back and forth with engineering because there's no documentation, figuring out [what] to do when the data changes or events are dropped, then wrapping all that context in a pretty bow and communicating it to stakeholders.*
>
> *Writing SQL and creating charts is by far the easiest 10% of an analyst's job. The other 90% is a thankless grind chopping through an ever-growing jungle of data debt. Unless THAT problem is solved, anything AI can do is just putting lipstick on a pig.[30]*

---

[30]https://www.linkedin.com/posts/chad-sanderson_dataengineering-activity-7090737104497889280-j89x

---

The other interesting take on AI in analytics relates to the evolution over time of the team structure. I was speaking to someone high up in AI at Google and they mentioned that originally the AI teams would consist of 3-4 data scientists trying to find the right pattern-matching algorithm, and then casting about for a data engineer to productionize it. Now, with the focus on AI and ML and the built-in support in infrastructure, you usually only need one data scientist and 3-4 Engineers – and in fact, the tools are making the data science part almost a commodity.

I asked if it was possible to cut all the data scientists out of the picture, if the tools existed that would allow a businessperson to plug into some sort of Universal AI where you plug in data and say: optimise for x. Bless them for not throwing things at me (I was effectively asking if it was possible to make him and his teams redundant), but he paused a second before answering.

"Even if that was possible (and we're not far off that), you would still need someone who would be able to define the metric."

I was a bit perplexed by that and said, "Surely that's obvious. It's sales. It's always sales."

He shook his head and said, "Is it though? Is it sales? Is it profit? If you optimise for sales of a particular product, you might be warping the contents of baskets that are much more profitable because of the other things that the customer is buying. Likewise, if you reduce the number of people buying a product, are you robbing yourself of the lifetime sales to that customer as they get what they want elsewhere? Does that enter into your calculations?"

I got it then. "Ah, so what you're looking for is not even a data scientist – more of a metric definer – you're looking for someone who has the ability to tease the answers to those questions out of the business, because the data science part is easy once you've got that."

"Well, I don't know about easy, but you're getting the idea."

Lastly, I'll leave you with this idea. AI looks like it is trained on content that is readily available, like website content and blog posts for example. AI is also used to *generate* blog posts and website content. In the same way that mad cow disease was caused by a closed loop of feeding the flesh of cows to cows, are we not making something similar by feeding AI generated content into the AI training content? Let's see if I can get #MadCowAI trending...

Some Workplaces Just Suck. Some People Just Suck

The thousands of words preceding this have been written (a little optimistically perhaps) about how things *should* be. You *should* have the opportunity for a raise. For a promotion. To learn new things and have more challenges. To do rewarding, meaningful work. To have honest conversations with your manager. To have regular check-ins during the year. To have goals and objectives. To work with people who do not undermine or backstab you. To work with good people who know their stuff, who you can trust to deliver what they say that they will in the time frame agreed.

But sometimes you don't. Sometimes your co-worker, your boss, your boss's boss or your stakeholder are problematic. Or incompetent. Or some sort of sociopath or psychopath – or any combination thereof. Sometimes there is no malice and there are relationships that simply start off shaky and never quite come right.

Sometimes, you have a team of two and you have three or more people's workload and then your co-worker gets a job somewhere else, and the expectation is that you will do all the work. And when you complain and argue and escalate there is still no relief.

Sometimes, you just have to recognise the warning signs and look after yourself and find something different to do. Or move on to a different workplace. And there is nothing wrong with that. Because sometimes, after all the talking and mentoring and training and coaching and development plans, sometimes you just have to be honest and say, "this isn't working for me."

You can sometimes get a feeling when you walk into an office. There's a level of anxiety you can pick up from the body language of the people you see around the place. Do they look harried? Are they hunched from carrying unimaginable weight on their shoulders? Are their faces lined from scowling? You can also get a feel for what the place is like from the answers to your questions in interviews.

Sometimes There Is No Answer

I would love to be able to give you a list of things to do in any scenario, that are guaranteed to work every time. This book is my attempt to outline to you the things that I think are important, based on my years of experience and my conversations with others, and then inviting people to challenge and discuss what I have written. But it might not match your experience. My advice might not work. How you interpret the situations you find yourself in, how you interpret my advice, and how you implement that advice might be all wrong.

And sometimes it seems like there is no answer.

But there usually is. Slavery is against the law in most jurisdictions. So, you do have a choice. And sometimes that might be taking a step backwards on the ladder, or into a different department, organisation or industry.

Sometimes there is no silver bullet, and you just have to bide your time. Ride out the bad situation. Hold on until the other person moves on. But please, find someone to talk to. At work or outside of work, have someone to vent to. And don't let the stress of your situation build up into an unhealthy reaction. Because no job is worth going to prison for. And talking to people and reading books are two of the best ways of identifying the best way out of bad situations.

Good luck! You can do it!

PART 8

The End

Summary

Thanks for reaching the end of the book! If you enjoyed it, please give it a review on Amazon or Goodreads.

We started off defining analytics. I introduced a way of measuring how good an analytics function is by thinking in terms of internal relationships: data, operations and political, and external relationships: IT and stakeholders.

I made a passionate appeal that it is not possible to measure ROI for analytics. I expect to get a lot of challenge on that chapter, and I imagine I will be writing a lot more in defence.

Then there were the guidance chapters. I tried to explain the drivers of culture that have the biggest impact on what kind of experience you may have in a job in analytics. I also tried to identify ways in which you could break into analytics.

Then, the bulk of the book: I looked at the things that matter in careers at three levels. I made the argument that the skills that get you into analytics aren't those that lead to a successful career. I further argued that one of the reasons there are so many bad managers is because you take people who are skilled in a technical field and then give them management responsibilities without the support or guidance that they need.

And finally, I had some fun with some provocative ideas.

I hope you disagreed with at least one part of this book. I hope that somewhere along the way you thought to yourself, "that doesn't match my experience." If I was able to sum up all the experiences possible in a whole industry I suspect that I would be writing in such vague generalisations that the book would have limited value. I make no apologies for that. But I hope you were able to get value from the other parts of the book.

I fell into analytics. I didn't study it in school. But I've always been adjacent to it. I grok Excel. I grok SQL. And when you inhabit such a space your natural curiosity goes a long way as a driving learning factor.

I find the culture of the workplace fascinating. In fact, it has been my attempts to make sense of environments that I have found myself in that has led to this book. The other driver to write this book was a genuine attempt to give back to an industry that has treated me well.

I want to take a second to wish you well on your career. However long you work in analytics, I hope you get to the point where you are able to enjoy a fair exchange of value for your time and efforts. I hope that you have a career full of opportunity with rewarding projects that are full of impact. May all your co-workers be people you can trust. May your managers lift you up, inspire you and support your growth.

Finally, for some more links and further reading, please check out https://cglambert.com/adventures-in-analytics-the-links/.

About the Author

C. G. Lambert is a consultant who regularly works with organisations identifying and rectifying issues with their analytics function. He spent seven years in webdev before converting the SQL part of that skillset into a fifteen-year analytics career in a broad range of industries, ranging from forensic data analysis to front page analytics responsibility for the Tesco website. His favourite data visualisation is modelling the impact of different recorded music contracts for MIC and the MMF. He holds a BA, an MBA and is a dual UK/New Zealand citizen. His other works are fiction, including a rom-com co-written with his partner and a fantasy series.

cglambert.com

www.linkedin.com/in/christopherlambert

www.ingramcontent.com/pod-product-compliance
Lightning Source LLC
LaVergne TN
LVHW032255060326
832902LV00024B/4598